TEIKYO WESTMAR UNIV. LIBRARY

⟨ W9-BMI-182

PICTURES OF PATRIARCHY

TEIKYO WESTMAR UNIV. LIBRARY

PICTURES OF PATRIARCHY

BATYA WEINBAUM

42-1825

South End Press
Boston

Copyright © 1983 by Batya Weinbaum

Copyrights are still required for book production in the
United States. However, in our case it is a disliked necessity.
Thus, any properly footnoted quotation of up to 500 sequential
words may be used without permission, as long as the total
number of words quoted does not exceed 2000. For longer
quotes or for a greater volume of total words quoted, permission from the publisher is required.

Library of Congress number 82-061150

ISBN 0-89608-161-3 paper
ISBN 0-89608-162-1 cloth

First printing in USA
Production by South End Press
Cover design by Lydia Sargent

SOUTH END PRESS   302 COLUMBUS AVE
BOSTON MA 02116

DEDICATION

As an old man lay dying, I grabbed him by the collar and I shouted to him, "Quick, in the last ten minutes before you go, what do you believe in?" He gasped, then muttered, "The last ten minutes before you die, you believe in..." and then he expired on me. Before I could say what I had been thinking—no, I'm not asking what I believe in, but what you believe in— not a universal truth, because we are different people

—dream, June 1979

WITH THANKS TO

Laurie Nisonoff
Frieda Werden
Katie Stewart
Support group at Room of One's Own
Molly Snyder
Cummington Community for the Arts
A Woman's Place

TABLE OF CONTENTS

PREFACE

"I THINK," MY friend announced, looking at herself in the mirror and proudly rubbing her belly which was barely covered by her bikini, "my body is ready to have a baby." We were vacationing in Southern Italy. Or rather, she was. She lives there. A leftover leftist from the student movement, she now teaches biology at the university. We had just spent the day visiting her mama and papa in Napoli. Back safely to her own home, this had been her opening remark to me.

I picked up a letter I had written to the man back home in New York, and began to read my correspondence to her loudly and slowly, so that she could think about the relevance the letter held for what she had just said to me.

> When I most strongly felt the desire to have a child I was standing in my kitchen. I had just scrubbed my floors. This was a couple of weeks after coming out of the hospital. I was still recovering, still partly sick. Must have been the second week of January. I had just learned from a woman's health book something that the doctor neglected to tell me: that infertility was a possible result of the infection of my tubes during surgery. A friend read this section of the book over the phone to me. I became hysterical and couldn't bear it. I hung up, saying I wanted to be alone, scoured my bathroom, scoured my kitchen, and, standing in front of my kitchen sink, began to reason rationally to myself: so, you'll adopt a child from Latin America, others

ix

have. Suddenly an explosion went off inside of me. The pang emanating from my internal organs was so sharp, so quick, that I couldn't stand on my feet. I rolled on my freshly scoured floor, gripping my gut in front of the exposed pipes of my kitchen sink. NOOO the flame uncurling within me shrieked, YOU WANT A CHILD TO BE AN EXTENSION OF MEEE— that's the point of all this learning, all this work. You want a child to extend this restless self-improvement effort beyond the boundaries of your self. The feeling, the thought, the attack, the desire, whatever it was, was so strong that one of my favorite gold leaf dishes fell from the sink above me and broke.

"Yes," painfully and pensively my friend answered me. "What you say in your letter is part of my desire to have a child at this moment of my life, I know." She turned from admiring her golden sandy belly in the mirror to gaze at me.

"And," I went on, returning her gaze steadily and letting the letter drop, "thinking about the problems you are having at this moment in your job at the university, the other side of the coin just occurred to me: why women feel that desire so strongly and men don't."

She tilted her head questioningly.

"I mean for social reasons, not just biologically," I said in response to her tense look. She relaxed and listened to me. "Men channel that need back into their work."

"But," my friend observed abruptly, interrupting my cross-continental reverie provoked by the conversation, "that's only men in certain jobs, not in most of them." With this she left off from the mirror and began to pace the floor in front of me.

"Ah, you caught me," I admitted. "The man I was thinking of was a small businessman. He reinvests his self-improvement observations into the management of his shops; and his grasp of character into the decision of whether or not to hire or fire a person. But it's not the job, as such," I insisted. "For instance a man in your job at the university would try to rearrange the research institute. He would expect, more or less, that his observations would be welcomed by colleagues as a responsible attempt to improve the common working situation. You, instead, voice complaints periodically and are never heard. In fact you are criticized for your attitude and feel punished; so you make the decision to spend as little time as possible at the institute, and you decide at once that you are ready to have a baby. Partly out of your frustration that your observations had no effect on the world around you. Being a woman, you can't channel your discontent into re-ordering the structure of work as easily. It's almost as if a cold gray barrel of cement faces you."

"Yes, I see the point you are trying to make."

"Which is what?"

"That you can't look at the social space as such," she answered seriously. "You have to look at the individual who occupies a given social position." She thought for a moment, and then concluded, "And that men and women might occupy their places of work differently."

"That's correct!" I exclaimed exuberantly. And then playfully, "'Congratulations. You made it into my theory book if not into my novel."

"I want both." She pouted, hurt.

I shouted at her, hurling a pillow across the room and finally leaping off the bed to attack her physically: "I CAN NEVER DO ENOUGH FOR YOU!"

She stepped aside calmly. I missed her, and fell to the floor muttering: my role is not to have an effect on the world, my role is merely to describe it...

Still, at thirty, most of my adult years have been motivated by the strong desire to make sense out of everything that has ever happened to me. This book represents a momentary level of understanding at least of that portion of those events which could be held in the above remnant of conversation: that men and women experience the world of work differently, so differently that it should be called the *sexual political economy.*

Before reading the book I want to prepare you with a guide to your/my/the journey. The book shares an ardent straining of both the process of trying to make sense of the world (as in the vignette we just read) and the resulting radical feminist theory. Part I (Development of Radical

Feminist Workplace Theory) elaborates my personal history, a good starting point, as I have been schooled in the women's movement on the principle that the personal is political. I try to show how the process of living my life in a particular political environment as a female, living a life which was somewhat unconventional, ultimately led to my radicalization and brought me to see the world in a particular way. My experience of the 1970s gave forth a radical feminist vision and the process of living under patriarchy led to the development of the paradigmatic vision of kin categories in the economy, the book's central thesis. As a young radical trying to enact beliefs equally with men, I found I couldn't because for women the world is not safe, and people don't hire women in the workplace or treat them equally. Thus our material condition affects or limits our idealism and pushes us to create an alternative reality—through creating our own visions, or through trying to create family.

Part II (Kin Categories in the Economy) states the sex and age role division of labor in the workplace as ideal types. I present the new paradigm for analyzing sex and age differences in the workplace in more detail, breaking down the categories along the characteristics of space, relation to work, relation to other workers, reward and skill. I suggest that workplace roles can be looked at in kin categories because people are in families at the same time that they are in the workplace. Besides, family is where consciousness at work comes from. I give an extended example from a particular workplace after the paradigm has been explored, and note how racism and other factors might intervene to place adult males in slots other than ones designed for the more privileged roles of the patriarchy.

Part III deals with modes of consciousness in the sexual political economic existence, showing ways of perceiving the world which come out of the dynamic between the oedipal family and the patriarchal structure of work. It is suggested that clinging to family roles is done by workers; that to overcome this we as women have to create a new culture and choose to instill a different consciousness within ourselves. Psychic symbolism is intuited to get to the bottom of how culture takes meaning for the actors. It lays the basis for the logic that leads to the leap that sexuality might be a revolutionary force used to subvert rather than support the cyclical process.

Part IV (Variations on Some Themes: Instances of Sexual Political Economy) consists of excerpts from my theoretical observation notebooks from a period in which, having developed this perspective, I saw "shots" or evidence of it everywhere. Often in teaching classes and running groups where I shared this perspective, others experienced this "seeing it everywhere" and they deepened their vision by keeping running notebooks too. Again, in being laid-bare about the process, I am including much of my own material from this time too. This inclusion is not meant to be linear but discursive, like contact sheets in photography.

As the 1970s ended, we left the most exciting decade in history for the development of feminist culture and theory. I am making this record to further this process, having faith that we can expect even more in the 1980s than any of us have yet been able to conceive. I think the more we socialize the usually private struggle which is part of the creative thinking process, the more aids will exist to support future feminist thinkers, no matter what issues the future society throws up for those women to grapple with intellectually. I also think that as times change and traditional sex roles re-surface, those future feminists will be more in need of such support. Consequently, those of us who have been straining to think in new ways in the 70s are even more obligated to make an effort to share and interact with those reading our books as starting points in the mid-1980s. For think of the gap: by the time our radically new visions have jelled, the social environment has once again settled down. As we develop the confidence that our radical new thoughts are indeed right and worth developing, the society becomes more conservative. A reminiscent walk through the Columbia University court-yard reveals not guards vs. students, but students who maintain the guard in themselves. Hence young readers and maturing feminist writers will be increasingly out of whack, out of sync, out of line.

Here is an attempt to align them.

PART I

DEVELOPMENT OF RADICAL FEMINIST WORKPLACE THEORY

1.
WHEN MY FIRST
book came out, a
young woman
came to see me. She asked why I wrote the book the way I
did, and did I think radical feminist theory could be developed in the university. I had given a lot of thought at the
end of that book to how new ways of thinking are developed and decided to begin addressing that question
directly.

The first book stated that since, as Marx proposed,
differences based on sex and age did not disappear as
members of each group joined the pool of collective labor,
to grasp workplace experience we had to diversify the
singular "worker" point of view by including sex and
relation to the household. I proposed that new categories
be defined: that the standard "individual worker" of
Marxism be called the *Father* to capture this adult male
worker's relation to the household, i.e., his relation to
other workers across sex and age lines. The proletarian
wife—or adult female—I proposed we call the *Wife*; the
single woman, the *Daughter;* and the young male, the
Brother. I chose the terminology *Brother* to emphasize
how young men band together to seize what they can get
(as in brotherhoods and unions), to stress that they did not
automatically inherit from the *Fathers* as sons. I chose
the term *Daughter* rather than sister to show how women
are isolated under patriarchy. Thus I had defined four
categories of individuals in relation to the household and
in relation to each other. I stopped the book, equipped to

1

trace the route of each through production and to distinguish among their variant economic existences. I also
wanted to explore the economic bonds made between the
various kin groups, *Father, Wife, Brother,* and *Daughter,*
and how these bonds were used to maintain economic
inequalities within classes.

This definition of the workplace in sex and age
specifics rather than general class terms, I argued, cleared
up a lot of theoretical and practical problems in political
history and movements for social change as well. In fact,
using these political economic categories to look at socialist economies could also assist in seeing why promises to
women were structurally unable to be realized. Once you
see the Marxist individual worker as the male, the *Father,*
you see the political organization of the proletariat as the
organization of the fathers too. I suggested that without
breaking down the economic basis of cross group pooling
in the household, we would never dissolve the extraordi-
nary power now held by prole-patriarchs in the state, the
unit which makes decisions about whether to invest in
daycare or weaponry. I suggested that each sex and age
group might pool its own income and resources and thus
lay the economic basis for developing a decision-making
state of its own, a unit which could operate without each
group having its separate physical or geographic territory.

The inspiration and support for this thesis came from
the feminist movement and radical political circles, not
from academia or traditional disciplines (such as economics and political science) which is the only form of
intellectual life the young woman who came to see me
knew. Her question made me think about the movement of
the 70s, my involvement with it, my education, and how
all of this gave me the freedom to innovate intellectually.
It was my involvement in progressive education that
allowed me to recognize the relation between form and
content and to develop a form other than a critical
academic one to generate this new radical feminist vision.

I attended a small college, new in 1970, constructed
according to the tenets of the movement for progressive
education. That such a college came to be at all has to be
seen in the context of the protests and riots that disrupted
the colleges in the 60s. As a 60s high school student, I had
watched the college protests on TV and with others had

formed the general impression that when one got to college what one did was take over the university and make the system relevant.

Many were ready to go to college influenced by this philosophy. We were often the high school innovators, iconoclasts, renegades, and rebels: we abolished student councils in acts of protest; we discontinued student newspapers when our articles about Vietnam, dress codes, and marijuana were censored. A concern spread to corporations from which administrators got their backing. In the late 1960s a plan for an elite ideal college was developed by such people; and in 1970 the projected "ideal" college opened its 250 slots to people like me.

When I went east to college, I had come from a provincial childhood in a small town in Indiana, though this town also felt the effects of the 60s. Our mayor was quoted in *Time* magazine as saying he had no intention of closing the red light district which stood near the state university. The opportunity for the boys to let off steam in this nearby red light district had, he thought, spared the campus from rioting. The boys were too busy visiting prostitutes to do any serious thinking about the draft, the relevancy of their education, or the unjust war being perpetrated by the American system.

Many were concerned with cooling student revolt. That's how my hometown mayor rose to national prominence. They (if one adopts the conspiratorial view of history) were grappling for any route other than the one which was clamored for—which was to stop the war and end inequities in the system. In a certain sense, my college was just another form of red light district: getting future campus protest leaders together and doling out permissiveness in education.

Whatever the confluence of political reasons and social forces, the ideology on campus was that the best kind of learning came from firsthand experience, that any particular theme could be approached from many modes of inquiry, that the more angles you took on your subject the more enriched your understanding of that subject would be. Peer input and non-expert evaluation were also essential components of learning. Hence the origins of my interdisciplinary learn-by-doing way of thinking allowed me as a feminist to synthesize from many areas what I read, saw, thought, heard, felt and learned in conversation, as well as what I researched or absorbed in lectures.

My passionate interest was photography. In this genre I learned artistic concepts, but I was also interested in the ideas of politics. I decided to specialize in learning to think politically by taking an extended field study in radical education and anarchy at another center of the progressive education movement, the CIDOC community. Run by an ex-priest, Ivan Illych, the Centro de Inter-cultural Documentacion was having a seminar on de-schooling society, offering courses by Paul Goodman, Carl Friedenberg, George Denison and other influential thinkers and leaders of the radical education movement who were gathering in Mexico. Besides being attended by North Americans, CIDOC was populated with the most radical of the revolutionary priests and nuns who had in some form or another, along with Paolo Freire and Camillio Torres, become involved in revolt in Latin America where they had been sent as missionaries. These people had thrown their lives into Third World liberation struggles. Surrounded by such models, those of us at the seminar came to believe that if one believed strongly enough in a philosophy, one changed one's life, and that if one succeeded in living according to one's ideals, one could have an effect on society.

The most radical position in this movement was anarchist: that it was a contradiction to build a "free school." If you were going to attend a school without walls that encouraged you to learn by going out in society, then you might as well leave the school entirely. Otherwise what you paid for was establishment approval. Thus the college I was attending was explained to me as a liberal cop-out. Supporting their arguments with quotes from Proudhon and Kropotkin, the CIDOC leaders encouraged us to drop out. So we did.

2.

I SAY WE. This decision was made with a friend with whom I had gone to CIDOC from college. That summer after withdrawing from school, we went our separate ways: he to New Hampshire to work in a resort, I to Mississippi to teach photography in a Jewish summer camp.

The deflating of my ideals began as I started to work. I had worked before as a recreation director in a government program, but only while living at home and not out on my own. When I got to camp, I found that I was to be a counselor. There I was, eager to put my photographic skills to use and be economically self-sufficient, only to find out that I was to be a glorified babysitter.

Midsummer I got a letter from my friend in New Hampshire encouraging me to join him in Boston in the fall. He planned to get a menial job and pursue acting while making films and writing poetry with other drop-out, beat, countercultural performers, writers and artists in the vicinity. His letter enticed me. In the fall I arrived on my friend's doorstep on Symphony Road.

My friend's letter sounded romantic but Symphony Road was a slum. Bound as we were by our mission to carry out Illych's principles, some major problems began to occur. The core problem for me was that I was not "one of the boys." I soon learned that making it on my own in the world was going to be harder for me because I was a woman. First, I didn't feel safe in my friend's cheap neighborhood so I had to get an apartment elsewhere. I didn't feel safe living alone either and soon I moved back to Symphony Road because I couldn't pay the rent. Second, my friend could earn more money being a short-order cook than I could as a waitress being paid only in tips. Third, even when I tried to look for work in photography, my self-proclaimed profession, I ran into problems. I was often told I couldn't have a job because I was a woman. At a museum I was denied a job as a photography assistant because they thought I couldn't lift statues; a modelling agency told me I couldn't entice the models sexually to photograph them for fashion portfolios. Even when I got a job printing in a darkroom, the manager used to come in and lay his hands on me. While selling film in a photography store in Harvard Square, the boys selling cameras earned more per hour than I did, in addition to making commissions. One of the older salesmen expected to kiss me on the cheek every morning, although that had not been in the film girl's job description. Also unwritten was that the customers expected smiles from me. I once made a mistake on a sign and to my humiliation the owner screamed. "YOU DIZZY BROAD," in front of the customers, treatment men making mistakes never received. I had to go to the basement to hide. Finally, my friend didn't get raped hitchhiking, the countercultural style of travel in the poverty of those days. But I did.

The rape was the most genuinely formative and radicalizing experience, but largely for sex role reasons of which this rape was the epitome. The idealistic principles along which I had modelled my life caved in on me. When I had no principles to make sense of my life, I disintegrated into raw existential terror and fright. From the depths of my complete emotional disorganization, something else rose up which I could only call my own resolve. The rape was a juxtaposition of my trying to be myself, being in the world and doing my work, and a devaluing of myself brought about by social forces. Lying in the car of a man who had also threatened murder, I tried not to see his head writhing between my bared knees. My eyes focused on the white snow hitting the windshield of his car and rolling slowly down into the dark winter night. All I could feel was focused in one vein: if I ever got out of that car, I would go far, very far, away. I vehemently cursed myself for letting silly social barriers get put in my way by a society I didn't believe in anyway. If I ever got out of that car, I swore out loud, I would pursue my work no matter what, even if I was a woman. These oaths took my rapist off guard. He released me.

Getting off alive, I did go far way, while I still had the will to act on my own resolve. The farthest place I knew was Chile, for far to me at that time meant distance, geographic space. I knew about Chile from Bulnes, a Chilean poet at CIDOC. As soon as I had worked long enough in the photography store to purchase equipment, I went to Chile by land down the edge of South America, photographing people who took me into their lives and writing stories of their struggles to sell to magazines on my return.

The stories of the people's struggle for survival frightened me as much as my own life did at the time. By the time I reached Chile, I was struggling for some comprehension, some order. I could not make sense of what I saw or heard. In a Bolivian hospital, two nurses drew me aside. One told me how accidents were created to maim dissidents in the mines; the other whispered how beds were empty because the place was only open to miners and they were afraid to come for fear of being drugged and poisoned. A troup of beggars accosted me on the La Paz Cathedral steps, led by a dwarf with no arms or legs being pushed on a roller cart by a little cross-eyed boy with bulging stomach and no ears. Doctors in Altplano villages played chess and ordered nurses to boil eggs while across the flaked, dry river bed the streets of smaller towns four miles away were strewn with the tolls of epidemics. I had seen bodies draped in black, lying on the ground of a courtyard of a small town. I had seen children running, afraid to cry. I had been approached by old men begging the Ministerio de Salud driver, who had chauffered me there, to come back the next day by jeep with the doctor to administer vaccinations.

I came to Latin America to escape terror and confusion; so far my adventuresome journey had only magnified both, made them deeper, touching off more in myself. I lay in bed in a hotel room alone, listening to "Mission Impossible" dialogue pumped in on the lounge TV, thinking I would be better off dead. If I could just get myself to Chile alive, perhaps I could order it all in my head. There would be people to talk to. I had names of people I had met at CIDOC. In Bolivia, I was all alone; voicing the questions forming in my throat drew silence and nervous blank stares from people in cafes, from government officials. Apparently, there had been a coup.

Chile in 1972 was in many ways a good society to walk through in search of order. There was disorder all around. Parafascist youth gangs were stalking the avenidas of Santiago with clubs. Each day a different demonstration: one with tractors and red flags against IMPERIALISMO; the next with people banging pots about COMMUNISMO. I would be interviewing somebody in the Ministry de Salud who would be telling me that any article I wrote had to make clear that abortion was available for health reasons, not to lower the birth rate. In the middle of the interview we all ran downstairs because of the earthquake. A German textile manufacturer would tell me that what was going on was just like Nazi Germany. I would be saying no, this is different, somehow.

Disorder, disorder...but everywhere, everyone was talking about *why,* and what they could do about it. This happened in nearly every conversation I had—with peasant women over abortion; with women in barrios over daycare; with students collecting information to disseminate in a North American newsletter; with students from Africa, Moscow, Brazil, the Philippines; with Christian Democrats in the Ministry of Education complaining about the Socialists; with Socialists in the Centros de Madres complaining about the Communists; with shopkeepers over supplies, shortages, strikes, prices; with a nun working in Valdivian slums (much like the radical Catholic church people I had met in Mexico) who gave me a copy of *The Feminine Mystique* and took me to visit houses where husbands beat wives, where daughters were pregnant, where sons had become drunk because they were unemployed.

I inhabited bookstores which were filled with Marxist literature. With every conversation I returned to the bookstore filled with questions. I sought answers among those irresistable books. However, some of my questions could not be answered even by reading the Marxist books. Especially those which came up in the conversations about women.

I went to the Women's Divisions at the party headquarters involved in the six-party coalition that had been democratically elected to the government. The people there were more leftist than those in the government. Although Allende had been elected president, the Socialist president inherited a bureaucracy filled with people from the last, more conservative government. Still nobody anywhere had time to talk about women, daycare or abortion. It was true that jobs were being developed for *campaneras.* Centros de Madres were organizing shipments of women's handicrafts from outlying towns to Santiago markets. Young women were volunteering for the year of service required of all 19 year olds but women went to health and educational facilities while men went to the army. Liters of powdered milk were distributed free to mothers to feed children and, it was said, this was being done for the women.

One night in frustration I asked an American student working in the barrios how I could find enough answers in my short stay to write articles to sell. I remarked that I had read an article by Paul Sweezy that he had written after only two weeks, so I should be able to do it, too. The second student told me, "Oh, well, he's a famous economist, he'd know important people to talk to. He could find out quickly what he needs to know." Then he showed me a radical economics publication of a North American organization. The issue he gave me was a special collection on women's role in the economy in which there was an article about women in another "socialist" state, the Soviet Union.

Here the student and I interrupted our conversation to move to the balcony. Below, we watched the fascists parade through the streets slashing tires, carrying torches. I was scared. But the fellow next to me on the balcony was an economist. He was also a Marxist. And he remained calm. I decided to return to the states, study economics, and become a Marxist in hopes that I, too, could learn to stand calmly overlooking chaotic situations.

3.

MARXISM DOES HAVE a way of ordering your past and cutting you free from it. I discovered this at about the same age as Martha Quest, the main character in Doris Lessing's *Children of Violence*. As she, propelled by left-wing books, moved to the city from the provinces, I moved to New York to focus on another mode of inquiry: historical research. I let library study consume me, straining to make sense of my independent "field work." In courses at Columbia, I looked for explanations of what I had discovered in Latin America. I explored not only Marxism and economics but a range of social sciences. Yet the deficiencies of the espoused social theories always made me return to reading Marxism as that set of ideas could make the most sense of the world to me. Yet through Marxism I could not learn about women—particularly about the structural reorganization which might lead to liberation. Here I noticed a tremendous gap between what I read and what I saw. The gap became so great a year later on a visit to Cuba that I put away photography. I didn't want to see.

I couldn't withstand the conflict between the ideas about women's liberation (women's participation in work would free them gradually) and what I saw through my camera (a clear photographable workplace division into sex roles, as pervasive as in Chile). I naively thought putting away the camera would solve the conflict for me.

Not having yet fully understood that even a government led by the principles of Marxism will recreate a patriarchy, I took seriously the only two explanations I could think of. First, that Cuba was a small country that had been reduced to the position of economic satellite and, therefore, was not able to find resources to change itself internally. And second, that only 15 years had passed since the Cuban revolution and changing society was, after all, a very gradual process. So, when I returned to the States after my trip to Cuba, I studied China, a larger country with 25 years of experience. Unfortunately, I still saw a huge gap between ideas about women and empirical facts, case histories, visitor's reports and statistics.

I was moving closer to creating a feminist framework which would reorganize all those facts for me, but I wasn't quite there yet. This final step occurred when I took stock of my political activities. There I felt again the divergence between the words that were being used as if they explained things and my firsthand knowledge. I felt this divergence most keenly as a member of the organization which published the journal the Marxist economist had given me in Chile. I organized with other women for populist and feminist goals. We argued that knowledge should not be bottled up in the university, that economists should go to the community and learn to be activists by working with people. We also advocated starting research collectives to write about contemporary economic issues. Because of this activity I was often called to give talks myself. These talks were increasingly based on questions generated while doing library research. In the library, questions formed in my mind about the function of sex and age division of labor. When I was confronted with an audience of women who wanted to understand the contemporary economic crisis, answers would come to me.

In my years spent active in politics, I often felt the discrepancy between the abstract and the concrete, between the conceptual and the literal. I felt this as a woman

organizing populist projects inside a left academic organization where I felt politically ineffective. Gradually I was
convinced that these problems stemmed from being a
woman in a male organization; that women arrive in the
political arena differently from men, and hence see the
political world differently. These differences stem from
the fact than men and women hold different positions in
society.

On the other hand, when I gave talks to women's
groups, audience reactions would affect me. When asked
to present an analysis, I articulated my growing understanding of how sex and age division of labor enforced a
pooling of income in the family structure where women
were dependent on men, and children on parents. This
was the economic element missing from Marxist analysis
of work and the economy. I drew diagrams on the black-
board as I spoke, illustrating how this pooling of income
across sex and age lines organized through the family
operated as a basic mechanism of accumulation in the
economy. As I spoke, the reasons why socialism couldn't
liberate women came to me. The state's accumulation
rested on this staggered division of labor based on pooling
of income in the household too. Often I was abashed when
this metahistorical analysis was reduced to a question
from a woman in the audience: "Should you let a man pay
for your dinner?"

At first I felt frustrated that my concepts went over
everyone's heads. Then I began to see that women were
taking something from these large schematic diagrams
that could help them understand their own lives. Once
pushed to this recognition, I felt that the only valid way of
thinking was one that could provide an adequate framework for this interaction between the conceptual and the
literal, for the flow between the abstract and specific. The
more my realizations drove me to this, the more frustrated
I became with left university politics.

4.
SUSTENANCE FOR DEVELOPING a framework
that could provide for abstract/literal interactions such
as these came from two sources: thinking visually, during

which process a new sense of conceptual relations began to grow; and moving over to all-women's politics. Via the process of consciousness raising as practiced in the women's movement, I was put in touch with imagery that clarified my growing vision.

In my Marxist-feminist group, we began with a go-round where women answered questions about individual histories. When discussion topics were selected, we would reflect on the relation between life and the spoken thinking. I was convinced that useful categories would have to weld in new ways what women discussed among themselves.

The convincing act was a comparison of two different weekends of presentations. In the first case, a group of Marxist women volunteered to give a presentation on women and work. The group prepared facts, statistics and reports on activities of working class women's organizations. The second group prepared a session on the family in a diametrically opposite way. This group asked us to break into small groups, and then gave each group a few questions. Each member took turns answering the same questions before the group went on to the second one. The questions concerned our feelings about our families. A different kind of report and process would clearly generate a different kind of theory.

I was moving to inductive reasoning—starting from the particulars to the general principles. As in photography, where I learned to photograph freely to discover images, I began to look for the decisive patriarchal moment—to stop the world in a moment of time to discover the crucial relation. I then began juxtaposing these disparate images. As in photography I had tried to construct murals and blocks of photos and individual shots to find connecting relations, so I started with the stories I heard from women or the relations I observed in the workplace and constructed the theory backwards from a host of disorganized insights and perceptions.

The group, which met bi-monthly, discussed personal experiences in psychoanalysis as well as the feminist use of psychoanalytic concepts. Thus I was introduced to yet another process and series of concepts. Writing an article for the economics journal about how sexual division of labor affected state accumulation in China, I developed a

block and went to a psychoanalytic therapist recom-
mended by a member of the group to work it through.
Encouraged to explore what was behind the objective
parameters of the situation, I elaborated the realities of
work, money, family relations and sexuality on a different
level in poetry, visions and dreams.

As I made this conceptual transition, guilt over
deserting radicalism hounded me. The more I thought
psychoanalytically, the more attention I paid to my inner
creative aspect and to the artistic influences around me.
The rationalization I developed to quell the conflict
between politics and art went something like this: radi-
cals and artists have in common the struggle to maintain
a vision in the face of a social disorder which denies it, a
struggle motivated by the desire to pass their visions on to
the rest of humanity. Art, defined as an outer piece of work
reflecting an inner part of one's being, enables the viewer
to reach a new and greater level of understanding. The
struggle to claim this kind of understanding, to see the
particular in an entirely new conceptual or creative
framework, is the goal of those involved in radical politics
and art. The psychoanalytic process seemed to offer space
for that struggle. I submitted to the process which brought
parts to the surface and offered a new quality of understanding. When I came to difficult places in writing I
turned, through various forms of association, to explore
what was coming up in myself; and eventually began to
see the relation between where I got "stuck" and the real
gaps in the artist's tradition of thought. Not only did the
psychoanalytic process get me over my block, but it
imparted new insights which I began to collect and
arrange over time into the resulting theory of the workplace. Because I found through revision, publication and
conversation that these insights helped other people
reflect and even come to understand experiences in a new
way, in a different context, I came to think of this social
theory as projecting a radical vision of art.

Guilt over deserting radicalism as defined by Marxism was also somewhat assuaged by continuous encount-
ers with an old friend from my drop-out days in Boston. A
jazz musician, beat writer and poet with literary heroes
Kerouac, Ginsberg and Beckett, he maintained a critical

stance towards a Marxism that, when put into effect, betrayed minorities, jailed homosexuals and outlawed jazz as a form of musical subversion. The notion of pooling income made sense to him as revolutionaries in the black community had also advocated economic self-sufficiency. Seeing that I was having difficulty articulating in the academic mode themes which made sense to him and to others, he suggested that I should try to write a novel *a la* French existentialists, who wrote fiction to illustrate their philosophy.

In free form experimental writing, I did just that, receiving sustenance from other sources. I had moved, by this time, to an artists' neighborhood in New York's Lower Manhattan. I was surrounded by people who took their internal visions seriously and covered their loft space with various exploratory projects. Although working in a different medium, I did that too, drawing inspiration and support from avant garde ideas, discussion of process, and intellectual artistic concepts. Since I lived downstairs from a jazz piano player and composer at that time, I often wrote to live music. I wrote rhythmic poetic dialogues and focused on small perceptual and emotional detail. We performed them often and I found a new audience: people who worked outside the university and who found that the improvised pieces spoke graphically and clearly about sex and work.

I tried to take insights gained from innovative writing back to the level of theory. I still had a sense of mission, which was to connect the debates about Marxism and feminism with my inner visions. I wanted to write a book which would raise understandings from specific cases—cuts on jobs interviews, empirical research on women in China—to a level of theory about the interaction of Marxism and feminism, to produce a framework about women, work, sexuality and the family. I had the evidence from economic consciousness raising that family relations controlled consciousness including, though not exclusively, consciousness at work. The evidence generated in those groups seemed to geometrically expand from the process of therapy. Thus equipped, I charted the ideas of Marxism and feminism. I made presentations at colleges and conferences, goaded by questions women asked me. I would come home and sit on the floor of my loft and, working with the interaction of the debates over the last hundred years as my upstairs neighbor clashed out dissonant chords, the categories *Daughter-Father-Brother -Wife* popped out.

5.

I FORMED A GROUP of various feminist intellectuals and organizers from around the Marxist-feminist circles, which gave me the opportunity to discuss the concepts with women who saw the struggle with Marxism as a struggle with the entire male patriarchal tradition. As well as having validating, inspirational and supportive interaction with members of this group, I was frequently confronted with the importance of holding on to my consciousness of being a woman. When I held on to that, I thought one way: I saw clear social barriers that I wanted to break even though I was a woman; when I disappeared into Marxist academic thinking, I spent time being confused about why those traditions couldn't explain women's position. If I were able to maintain the consciousness of the moment I was raped, it seemed to me, I would attain an irreversible clarity which this group sustained in me.

I had begun to see the theory as art—like poetry, an expression of an essence. The theory I was writing at this time was also a crystalization of my own experience. I was walking around basically in two different worlds—in the world of work and in the world of the family—when all the flashes began to explode in me. I had the experience at this time of looking for work on the basis of carefully prepared resumes each slanted a different way, each a different version of who I was. I had cashiered; waitressed; modeled; gone to summer camp; sold film, soap, newspapers; done movement jobs and social work with children. But I had never before sought work on the basis of my accomplishments. Looking for work in this excruciating way, I began to feel quite solicitous. I was used to being able to dress down, like a student, out of the sex role. Now I had to learn to flirt and dress up i.e., to behave as job interviewers expected, according to imposed sex roles.

I found work in two different places—in a Christian bureaucracy and in a women's program at Brooklyn College. Moreover, I was simultaneously dealing with my grandfather. He was in a nursing home in orthodox Jewish Brooklyn following a cataract operation. Later I visited him in his apartment. So I was going in and out of disparate family and work worlds that reflected the starkest difference between cultures and I was forced to create the commonalities in my own mind. The days would be a whirlwind of getting up, going to work, and going to the grandfather.

As the workplace imposed a sex role, so did the grandfather, not only in how he related to me personally but also in the institutions which he began to share with me. For example, sitting in a synagogue which he took me to, family roles were made lucid. Fathers were called up to *davin.* * The fathers had wives who were organized into sisterhoods. Daughters could *davin* from lone slots up in the balcony but they couldn't enter the father's ritual as could the brothers. I would walk into my workplace at the Christian bureaucracy the next day and I would see the contours of the same kin category structure. *Fathers* ran offices, met with each other and trained younger workers— the *Brothers; Daughters* were hired for part-time short term jobs, primarily to be sent on errands like gathering documents from the library, much as my grandfather had sent me to the drug store for insulin. Although I was "hired on" as a *Daughter,* I would never be "brought in." Whatever the particulars of the structure I looked back over, the workplaces of my life and this pattern became vivid and clear to me. When I had worked in the camera store as a film "girl," I was sent to the post office; the salesman across from me learned from the *Fathers* who ran the shop, and trained younger male workers who earned more than me. The *Brothers* would rise in the field; as a *Daughter,* I would not.

Family roles, or the kin categories, seemed to be the basic formation that, multiplied a specific number of times, produced the given patriarchal structure of work. The family was the basic, fundamental chord on which

---

*pray

the workplace in adult life was structured. But how to articulate this consciousness of the root?

6.

WITH THE SUPPORT of the group and grants, I completed the writing of my first book, *The Curious Courtship of Women's Liberation and Socialism.* This was my feminist critique of Marxism and an analysis of social revolutions in terms of kin categories. But when I ended that book, I continued to work on the theory, clarifying the implications of the categories in other areas of life.

At this time, I had some grant money left and was down to one part-time job working in a government-funded program for women at Brooklyn College. This job gave me flexible time to work on theory and it also gave me a feminist context that supported discussion of principles. Another set of involvements I maintained over this time was with a group of women I had worked with at the Christian bureaucracy. This group was connected to Paolo Freire whose book *Pedagogy of the Oppressed,* used by Latin American Catholic revolutionaries, had also been popularized in radical academic circles. I needed the challenge of a constant audience to refine my concepts, and over the years this women's group provided it. I was asked many times to speak and help organize and plan conferences.

Because the patriarchal order of the churches is named very clearly, feminists in churches were more accepting of a theory based on sex, age and family roles than many. In universities, you have deans, after all; in churches, you have fathers. In department offices, you have secretaries; in Catholic orders you have sisters. Not only because of familial symbolism in daily rituals, professional church-related women had less of a leap to go through in accepting workroles according to kin category characteristics.

In working with the project on Women, Work and the Economy, the test in presenting the theory was not "how does this violate traditional ways of thinking on this subject?" but " how do we put this into practice to benefit all women?" I was working with activists with whom I shared some common radical assumptions. The Freire group operated their educational conferences along certain principles. The basic idea is that through dialoguing ideas are forged *with* and not *for* the oppressed. The central problem was: how can the oppressed as divided beings participate in the pedagogy of their liberation?

As presented in *Pedagogy of the Oppressed*, there is a relation between the given objective fact and the perception we have of that fact. I had defined the themes and improvised spontaneously; what I had to do was define the subjective/objective interaction with people. I asked women at conferences to tell their economic histories over three generations, and in their current lives as well. As I listened, I picked up certain information and then played it back carefully, showing how going in and out of economic participation in the workplace was defined by position in the family. This testimony contributed to the background of the theory: the history of capitalism, the rise and fall of certain forms of economic organization, the way groups of people are organized through families so that if one individual in one sex and age category isn't earning, the other is. Then I had to develop the foreground or elucidate how any job or individual role in the workplace could be seen against the backdrop of the historical theory.

That was what I set out to codify: the foreground, the way family relations at work affect daily lives. I listened to people tell stories about different jobs they had held and, in so doing, I learned to isolate characteristics. The image for me was similar to the physical process of isolation in belly dancing. First you learn how to move your shoulders, then your midriff, then your hips; then you put all the isolated movements together and dance. As I listened, I isolated the different crucial characteristics that seemed to define jobs: space, relation to work, relation to other workers, reward and skill. In a sense I organized, or codified, the testimony working in an oral tradition.

The vision refined in this way took hold of others besides me. I worked with a group that I had met through an organization that had research money from the federal government to look at the employment needs and opportunities of women in a certain geographical area. I was hired as a consultant to do staff training and while working with them I further organized a grid of characteristics to explain the categories. Soon the women in the group were thinking this way without me, even to the point of going out with a camera to photograph the work roles that they could see so clearly. Later I worked with a filmmaker and other photographers and had the opportunity to observe the roles in workplaces in China.

Thus starting from feelings and intuitive perceptions I had created a tool or method of workplace organization which others took up and used objectively. The theory became, as it is now, something separate from me.

PART II

KIN CATEGORIES IN THE ECONOMY

7.
NOW THAT WE
have shared a common understanding of the process, I will move on to presenting how sex and age differences manifest themselves in the workplace. This next section of the book will present in synopsis form the kin categories developed to analyze the sexual political economy. Then, after an example to place the image in your mind and some clarifications on usage and perspective, we will distinguish each according to space, relation to work, relation to other workers, reward and skill. The next step will be to explore thoroughly how this framework manifests itself in a single situation.

One thing you will learn as you go along is that any particular job cannot be identified solely on the basis of a single characteristic. Indeed you have to "feel" a certain job out, thinking about the context, the relation to other workers and the larger workplace structure beyond the particular situation. A specific job might have a cluster of *Wife*-like characteristics, but not all of them. The roles (*Daughter, Father, Brother, Wife*) should be thought of as exaggerations, ideal types, standards to measure away from, to measure by degree of divergence in the actual situation. Sometimes I think of them as interchangeable lenses to focus on different aspects of a situation; as characters in a novel. Nobody is really as gruff as Scrooge or as footloose and brave as the spunky dyke, Molly Bolt, in Rita Mae Brown's *Rubyfruit Jungle* but both characters do aptly capture and express certain perceptions and feelings eeked out dialectically in interaction with a predictable (here idealized) structure.

The objective parameters of sex and age division of labor in the workplace are as follows:

The Daughter. The worker in this role moves around a lot from job to job, taking and finding mostly short-term work which might be hourly, weekly or seasonally. In the workplace she usually does not have a space to call her own. Her pay is insufficient for self-support and obviously insufficient to support others. She exercises rote tasks on command rather than exercising judgment or taking overall responsibility for task completion. She often works under a workplace *Father* who issues commands. She is often required to use the skills of heterosexuality on the job—attractiveness, flirtation, seduction—if not actual performance of the act.* *Daughters* are to be seen and not heard. When not being sex objects, they must be invisible, like a backdrop or scenery.

The Father. By contrast, the worker in this role, usually an adult or older man, expects to enjoy stability along with consequent economic security. He accrues a feeling of being at home in the space which he personalizes in his years of employment in the same job. He receives more benefits, commissions and perks than other workers. His pay is sufficient for self-support as well as support of others. He often has his own area of responsibility and, in the hierarchy of work, he has the responsibility of determining and directing the tasks of others. Even if he does not, the pace of the workplace *Father's* work tends to generate the tasks of other workers. He acquires knowledge, expertise and skills in the course of his working life. He also interlocks skills with groups of *Fathers* within and beyond the individual workplace. His identification with the larger group of *Fathers*—management, the union, the state—is frequently stronger than his identification with other workers.

---

*See Part III for an analysis of the creation of compulsive heterosexuality on the part of the *Daughter* in the workplace role.

The Brother. What distinguishes this worker, usually a younger man, from all the rest is his expectation of rising within the workplace with the hope of moving into the *Father* category if he adequately performs his job. Unlike *Daughter, Brother* assumes he will work in the same place of employment for a number of years once he decides to take a particular job. While there, he is learning the ropes from the workplace *Fathers,* frequently organized as on-the-job training. Sometimes the training occurs in more informal buddy-buddy mentoring situations under the guise of other patriarchal organizations (such as sports). The accumulation of this worker's knowledge raises him into a better negotiating position if he chooses to bargain himself up the hierarchical ladder. His pay is sufficient for self-support, although he is not immediately able to finance the support of others. He is highly competitive with other workplace *Brothers* to see who will rise, who will get the biggest raise, the better offer, or the greatest benefits of continuous perseverance and employment.

The Wife. The worker in the *Wife* role (presumably the older married woman) performs her task in a space that is often separated from the other workers. If not physically separated, often she is isolated from others by the nature of her task. For example, it frequently falls within her duties to discipline the others to follow the rules of the establishment. The *Father* decides the rules; she carries them out. The workplace *Wife* uses her household management skills rather than area-related skills (as do *Father* and *Brother)* or the skill of sexuality (as does *Daughter).* It is not that the *Wife* doesn't learn anything at work, but that her workplace functions are analogous to those performed in the household: stocking shelves and ordering materials, the way the wife in the family is responsible for filling the refrigerator, pantry and closets.

She is a small parts or maintenance person tidying up after the work of others or laying the basis for others to complete a task of greater specialization. Her job is often dependent on the existing state of affairs in other facets of production. Her job is typical of that given to a married woman returning to work after raising children. As such, she experiences a disjuncture rather than an accumulation of skills. Her pay is not sufficient for self-support as it is assumed she is pooling her income with others—the welfare mother or working class housewife who might be hired on for a few days when an outlet store in a national chain is closing.

8.

FIRST TO ESTABLISH the kinship categories visually let's look at the dentist's office I used to go to. Five people worked there. The *Father* was the chief employer. He had his own space, his own office, his name on the door embossed on a gold plaque. His choice of paintings was on the walls so he had a personalized space to work in. He had stability, a permanent job. The pace of his work generated the work of others: he decided when to hire another dentist, the number of receptionists, assistants, whatever. He had power over others and respect for his occupation. The plaques on the walls credentialized his professional training.

The *Brother* (the dentist I went to) was the junior partner. He did not work in a group space in this situation but expected to move up either to a senior partner, to negotiate a better position elsewhere or to open his own office. He competed with the older dentist in the firm over who got and kept the most number of clients and with other dentists in professional associations who could always be hired to replace him as well.

The *Wife* had her own space isolated from other workers. She sat behind a window overlooking the waiting room. She laid the basis for others' work by scheduling appointments. She disciplined the others to follow the *Father's* rules, frequently entering the workspace to tell the hygienist or assistant (in the presence of the patient) to hurry up since other patients were waiting.

The assistant was the *Daughter* who had no space of her own to work in. She was in and out of both the dentists' and the hygienist's offices. She worked directly under one of them and they issued her commands: get this tool, do these set-ups, get such and such chart. The assistant did not earn enough money for self-support. Her work was part-time and temporary if not seasonal. She had no area of her own responsibility and no opportunity to work with other workers. She was non-skilled except insofar as she was to call upon the skills of her sexuality—to be a nice girl, a sweet girl, a good and comforting personality. She had to disappear or withdraw from the scene, to be a backdrop until the dentist needed her.

The hygienist was in some form a *Daughter* and yet a *Brother* too. She had her own space when she was at this particular office, yet she was only there two days a week and two days a week somewhere else, one day elsewhere, always coordinating appointments at the different dentists she worked for. Still, her skills did give her the ability to negotiate. And she had her own area of responsibility in which to exercise those skills. She was not docile or subservient. She could also be seen as a *Wife* in that her work was accessory production. She cleaned teeth rather than fixed them.

This example illustrates how the categories are flexible and may or may not apply in every situation to the ultimate degree. They have to be used insofar as they apply rather than as an argument around a situation. The hygienist was divided from the *Daughter* because she had some technical skills. Although she moved around, her knowledge in the dental industry raised her to a better negotiating position. She was, in fact, organizing a union to improve conditions and pay for hygienists in the dental industry but she related to the dentists through a professional organization rather than as an organizer in the office. The result of her organizing activity would only improve her own situation, not change the work relations at the office.

Now for some clarifying points about usage and perspective before we proceed. First, I focus on sex and age as the primary factors in this analysis and subsume class and race under them, breaking down traditional Marxist categories which have been illuminating in terms of class but largely sex blind. Sex and age are other factors which intervene in class and race. I have selected sex and age here as the primary lens of analysis since we often have no theoretical ways to think about them and since they do affect our primary mode of consciousness as long as the family is the primary unit and larger structures are generated by this. Variations on how to apply this nexus in different class and race situations appear throughout. There is obviously much more work to be done to apply this beyond the micro-level. For instance, work might be done to see how the necessary wage rate of the *Father* is lowered by pulling the *Wife* in and out of jobs according to the vicissitudes of capitalist crisis and machinations by the state. Rather than incidental to an analysis of capital, such a point of reference might show how keeping people in these sex and age related slots facilitates the accumulation of capital on the corporate, state and international level.

An added point can be made about kinship categories in relation to class. The further down you are on the class bracket, the less of the *Father's* characteristics you have on the job. Some "working class" jobs are *Brother* roles because as the class of capitalist *Fathers* rose, they took some patriarchal rights away from other *Fathers*. Working class men are disenfranchised *Fathers* who want their wives and daughters back in the home safe from the capitalist *Fathers* who overpower them.*

Another clarification to be made here is that the categories themselves may appear static. In practice they are not. The categories represent both an objective description of the workplace and a subjective experience of workers who fill these slots. A biological *Daughter* might behave or feel like a *Daughter* even when she is in a potentially *Brother* slot; and an adult male will relate to a *Daughter* slot quite differently if he should find himself in one—as large groups of fathers do in specific ethnic groups and under certain historical conditions. These differences in attitude and behavior stem, I maintain, not from a biological basis, but from the way sex and age roles are learned within the early family. Even if traditional sex roles are mitigated by progressive attempts within the individual family, or subcultural pockets which subvert or even appear superficially to reverse the patriarchal struc-

---

*The prole-patriarch (the revolutionary organizer of brotherhoods, communist parties, nationalist revolts) is also interested in restoring more of the father-like privileges at work, restructuring the public as well as the private patriarchy to suit himself.

ture, other social structures—like organized religion—
imprint the traditional sex roles quite vividly. Thus, when
differently sexed and aged individuals appear in the
workplace structure, they are unconsciously geared to
gravitate towards certain slots, even if those in power
aren't pushing them. And of course, they are more likely to
exhibit sex and age typed attitudes and behaviors in support of the enlarged patriarchal structure rather than
ones that subvert or explode it.

So it must be remembered when looking at the characteristics that these are social, not biological categories. To
explain what I mean I am going to use the society-as-
girdle concept. Yes, my hips have curves, but the society
emphasizes them to the point where I can't breath, can't
walk. The social has become a cruel distortion of the biological. The social, in fact, takes off on its own to the point
where it is possible that a biological male might occupy a
job which has traditional female characteristics—just as
a male can buy and wear a girdle or dress in drag and
work as a female impersonator. The difference is that
when most adult males take jobs which have socially
female characteristics—such as the inability to rise within the structure—they usually don't want to. What they do
under the best of historical conditions is develop a political consciousness, organize and try to do something to
re-align their patriarchal position. But other alternatives
are available: tranquilizers, heroin, dope and sadistic
power relations in which men assert over women the
power they see other "bigger" men get at work.

I might also add that this is a picture of the sexual
political economy of patriarchy taken squarely from the
Daughter's slot. This makes the theory highly unusual, as
most social theory is written from the point of view of the
Father, including, as I have said, the social theory of
class. Here the *Father/Daughter* interaction is the crucial, the essential dynamic. It is no accident that those two
roles are delineated more clearly than *Brother/Wife*. The
fact that *Father/Daughter* is the nexus came about in the
following way. Part of my reasoning was to find a psychological basis to go from feeling level to objective structural
analysis. I found and used Freud, noting how the Freudian psychological theories and categories were derived
from an oedipal basis. The subject at the bottom was the

Box 1: New Perspective Underlying Kin Category Father/
Daughter Nexus

Mother—her husband (his father)
│   as competition to revolt
son   against
           Daughter, his sister,
           not in view

TRADITIONAL VIEW

Father—his wife (her mother)
↑ \   a subject to feel
daughter \ deprived of
           brother: receiving
           mentoring from father
           and preferred/
           advantaged attention
           from mother

son, in Freud's view, who looked up and saw as his object, the mother. The father appeared as the mother's husband, whom he— the son, the actor—was jealous of and ultimately revolted against. The little girl as subject from which to form consciousness never came into Freud's view in any of his psycho-historic statements about world developments and social origins. So I attempted to reverse this and start with a daughter's consciousness and have her look up and see the father; and then the father's wife, of whom she was jealous. This mother (the wife) entered into the picture only as competition. But in so doing I found that I couldn't drop the little boy (the brother) as completely as Freud had dropped the unformed consciousness of the little girls who would grow up to be women. The brother too entered into competition with her, receiving more attention from the father than she did, as the father was imparting his position to his son, her brother. Since the little boy's relation to the girl and the way this relation formed her consciousness was crucial to me, I kept him in the picture as the brother. All of this is developed in Part III. It is clarified diagramatically in Box 1.

One last clarification. It should not be assumed that "real" i.e., biological daughters never have skills or accumulate knowledge. The point is, even if some women know a lot, they seldom get to exercise that knowledge because all that is open to them is the *Daughter* slot. It is not that women ever take their work seriously but that they seem to be always underemployed, segregated and objectified. This in itself produces the alienated attitude that becomes aligned with what is instilled, offered, opened or closed at the door of work, even if the *Daughter* through political struggle and other forms of altered consciousness overcomes what society has geared her toward. Think of the objective situation which produces this response not as the fault of the *Daughter* but as an attempt to subvert the structure with the only power she's got. Later we will explore how a defense against terror and mundane lives leads people to stay in the roles provided by the family dynamic.

9.

THE SCHEMA FOR ANALYSIS of workplace relations thumbnailed previously is outlined on the grid below. Here we can see *Daughter, Father, Brother, Wife* contrasted according to space, relation to work, relation to other workers, reward (material and non-material) and skill.

SCHEMA FOR ANALYSIS OF WORKPLACE RELATIONSHIPS

CATEGORIES OF ANALYSIS
1) Space; 2) Relation to work; 3) Relation to other workers; 4) Reward (*material, **non-material—status, fulfillment, psychological reward, privilege, and identification); 5) Skill.

DAUGHTER	WIFE
1) No space (waitress)	1) separated and isolated space
2) temporary, migratory, seasonal; accepts dictated tasks; performs by rote	2) small parts, dependency, cleans up or lays basis for others' task completion
3) docile, receiving; no team work	3) disciplines other workers
4) *not enough wage for self, not enough to support others; *good/bad girl identification	4) *not enough to support self expected to be supported by others *false identity with employer; boss's wife syndrome
5) non-skilled; or exercises aspects of sexuality as a skill itself	5) domestic skills; disjunction of skills

BROTHER	FATHER
1) group space, common area	1) personal space (executive suite, cab of truck driver)
2) expected permanence, move up in the hierarchy, ability to negotiate a move elsewhere	2) stability (tenured professor); own area of responsiblity
3) competition to move up	3) pace of work generates work of others
4) *enough wage to support self; expected in the future to support others *pleasure of climbing, winning	4) *enough wage for self and and others *power over others; respect for occupation
5) skills trained on the job prepared to move up in position	5) accumulation of skills, knowledge, expertise, interlocking skills—extension beyond individual workplace linking to others

10.

SPACE. What typifies the *Daughter* job in terms of space is lack of it. She never gets a space to call her own on the job. An archetype of this is the waitress in a restaurant. She runs around among the tables and the ever-bustling clientele as they eat in her temporarily assigned station. In many instances she is competing or rotating with other waitresses on a serve-as-they-come basis as new customers come in to be served. Another example is a "runner" employed by a medical laboratory to "run" the results of a test to the doctor who is sometimes in the middle of an operation. A "flyer" is someone in a department store who is rotated from department to department to cover holes created by sick leave or lunch hours on various floors. Then there is the Kelly Girl, sent by the agency to be a floating receptionist. At the National Council of Churches one of the full-time jobs of a particular woman was to move from floor to floor while the other receptionists took breaks or went to lunch. And, an example from industry is one of the textile mills I visited in China which had a job (filled by a woman) called a "threader." Her chair was on wheels tracked to the floor. The automated tracks moved her back and forth along the rows while she threaded the spools on the machines. In all these examples, the spaceless aspect of the *Daughter's* job is the key unifying aspect.

These *Daughter* jobs contrast strongly with the kind of space allotted to the workplace *Father*. He gets a private space, one he can personalize to the point where he feels at home on the job. He brings expressions of his personality into his work environment. The epitome of this workspace characteristic is the private suite of a business executive who has black leather couches and wall-to-wall carpet in his private office (in addition to the possible bar, private shower, change of clothes, etc.). To *Fathers* elsewhere in the class bracket lesser degrees of this personalized space are still granted. And the degree to which these *Father*-like characteristics are granted to workers is usually the degree to which they consider themselves superior to other workers and identify with the Bigger *Father*—and consequently the degree to which they are prevented from developing class consciousness.

The evidence of this will grow as we move through the material, but consider, for example, the truck driver—a trucker can decorate his permanently-assigned cab with girlie pictures just as the executive can put pictures of his wife alongside pictures of his mistress if he so chooses. He can do so because he has his own private space. This differs radically from the space of the girls in the typing pool back in the office.

In the area of space, you can see how different people fill their slots with their own modifications of the objectively assigned characteristics. I saw this when I worked in an office with an open middle room that had three desks arranged in a semi-circle facing the center. Around this middle room each member of the professional staff had his or her own private office. One time a professional was hired for a year and no additional private office space was available. He was given one of the three desks facing the center of the office. This professional proceeded to turn his desk around so he had his back to the center of the room—unlike the secretary and the receptionist. They, by the nature of their work, were required to face the middle. This temporarily displaced *Father* put a picture of his daughters in front of his desk on the wall; and thus, even visually, he could remind himself of his true role.

The same dynamic was apparent when I visited a stuffed animal factory in Brooklyn. In a large open room, a platform of men, most of them of Third World origin and not very fluent in English, sat turning the sewn animals inside out so that the men in another room could stuff them. Here you could say that this platform of men, in terms of space, were in a *Daughter* position due to the intervention of other factors such as race, unfamiliarity with language and the dominant culture, and imperialistically-created unemployment of the Third World which forces people to migrate to centers of economic development. In one corner of the room was a younger man. He was black but fluent in English because he had been born here. His job was to paint whiskers on the faces of black and yellow striped tigers after other men had turned them inside out and stuffed them. This man worked in a private corner, all alone, his back to the rest of them. He played a transistor radio loudly to block out the noise of the factory. He helped create the illusion for himself that he had pri-

Box 2: Father's Personalized Space a Privileged Position To Be In

In a Chambers Street greasy spoon, a man is watching the world series on television in the back. A driver stopping for coffee gestures to the cook who is working in the back and calls, "That's what it's like to be an executive!" The waiter at the counter with no space of his own listens to the world series on the radio along with the customers.

vate space to work in, e.g. he had carved out a *Father* characteristic (see Box 2).

A third kind of space I call *group space* or *common territory* of the *Brother*. A good example is a silk screen factory in Brooklyn where patterns are screened onto linens and shirts. When I was walking through this site, I noticed how the space seemed to divide the different kinds of workers. At one end of a long piece of machinery a woman sat putting piece after piece of white cloth on a vibrating belt which came out the other end imprinted with colors. There another woman sat removing the pieces of material one by one and placed them on a rack. Behind this machinery, against a wall under a window, was a living room area. This area was decorated with a radio and a couch. Three male workers sat socializing and relaxing. They were on "down time," as only at certain moments are their skills required to tend the machinery. Occasionally one of them got up to go tend a machine, but the majority of the minutes in their workday appeared to be spent in this casual interacting in a common territory. I saw a similar arrangement in a silk and dye factory in China. Here the women workers were playing the role of hand dyers—walking along the racks with a hand-held screen to apply the colors to the white material. And the men, in one corner which had automated machinery, were on "down time" congregated in a space tending a machine while one solitary woman worker fed it. Thus the men in this job had group space while the women worked separated and isolated from each other.

We can see this common territory or group space of the *Brother* in an advertising agency where they have a group space referred to as the "bull pen." Common practice is for each of the newly-hired illustrators, drawers and inkers to be given a stall in a big room where he sits drawing with his back to the other *Brothers* in a common area. The work they are given comes from a design made in the art department up above. This group territory makes the *Brother* job in the advertising agency similar to that of "downtimers" in the various notated factories; some *Brothers* never get out of the group space, never rise.

And then lastly, in terms of space, we have what I call the "separate and isolated" space of the *Wife*. Return with me to the Brooklyn silk screen factory. When the second woman

Box 3: Father's Personalized Space Crucial To Father at Work
At a community mental health center, the white male director made at least $75 thousand and had an office on the top floor. He had decorated it with plants, pictures, plaques awarding certification for his accumulation of skills. He had several secretaries working for him, and he felt so much at home at the office that he left a pair of soft soled mocassins to slip into when he got to work. On the other hand, the predominantly black security guards had central offices on (continued next page)

lifts the dyed materials off the belt to put on the rack, this rack is rolled into a separate room where one woman works all by herself. There she simply lifts the material off the rack and puts it on the dryer. She works, as the space emphasized, separated and isolated from the other workers. How is her separate space different from the *Father's* personalized space?: In the degree of control she has over her work environment. As she hung up the dyed material on the dryer, she was hit by exhaust and fumes. Furthermore, she had the noise of the machinery constantly with her. This was in stark contrast to the *Father*, the designer. He had his own studio elsewhere in the factory replete with tools, drawings, plants and a stereo playing his favorite music.

Another way in which the *Wife's* separated and isolated space differs from that of the *Father* is the amount of privacy given to the worker. The *Wife* hanging material on the dryer was interrupted constantly by people rolling in racks laden with new materials. The *Father*, on the other hand, was seldom interrupted. In Latin America, for example, male butchers stand together selling meat behind a counter while the cashier (usually a woman) sits in a little gold cage. She is separated and isolated from other workers but her space is far from private. At any moment a customer will come up and stick a receipt into her cage.

the basement and first floor. The guards were required to tie inmates when needed. Their reward was $6000 a year. They were told how to dress, as *Daughters* are. They wore black boots and worked in full view of the front door sharing a space with the receptionist. They did have a van to drive to inspect the grounds that gave them a sense of perusing territory. They also had a beeper which connected them with the director.

Furthermore, her cage is visible to the public. This makes the *Wife's* space considerably different from that of the *Father*.

11.
RELATION TO WORK.

One who never gets a place to call her own frequently also has a relation to work which is temporary, migratory or seasonal. The temp help girl epitomizes this *Daughter's* relationship to work. She goes here to be a receptionist, there to be a typist, to yet another place to file cards. She may never return to the same place of employment. You can see the logic of the employer: why bother to give her a space of her own given the temporary nature of the job?

Yet along with being temporary, migratory or seasonal is the seemingly resultant factor that the person who takes this sort of job has no expectations of rising within the workplace structure. She who enters a Madison Avenue advertising agency as a one-day stand receptionist doesn't necessarily imagine that one day she will become an illustrator or advertising executive. It is true that many are sucked into *Daughter* jobs that profer the illusion that they will work their way up (at least to marrying the boss), yet chances are that *Daughter* won't— even if she answers the phone unflinchingly, cheerfully and with the correct information. Likewise, a migrant farmworker roving according to harvest season cannot expect to one day own the machinery. This shows how racism interacts with patriarchy putting minority men along with women into the *Daughter* category.

The *Daughter's* relation to work, then, is usually to enter the workplace on a short-term basis to accept and exercise rotely assigned and predetermined tasks. This she often does as a routine performance without any personal application. Why should she bother to think about the work if she has no option to stay? This relation to work also leads to a subtle attitude of resistance. Why should

36

she apply herself seriously if she has no ability to create an expanding future there? Of course this resistance and the errors resulting from lack of motivation to pay close attention to boring unchallenging tasks is often read as: she's a dizzy broad, irresponsible and stupid. This short-sighted interpretation is made without examining how the opportunity to exercise responsibility and thought has been systematially removed from the *Daughter's* work by the division of labor organized by the employer himself.

As to the degree of impingement upon the worker, it is quite severe and seriously affects the slotted individual. It seems employers do take this into account. In my short foray into the social services as a professional, I talked with a woman whose job was to find employment for the mentally retarded or what we in the movement would call "differently abled" people. She reported that McDonalds was the best employer of these people because it was diffi-cult to keep anyone else slotted in the rote 8-hour day position of French-fry turner. The logic of the division of labor within the patriarchy has gone so far that capital-ism's international corporations' ideal worker is one who is presumed unable to think at all whether for organic or environmental/institutional reasons. I discussed this phenomenon with a check-out woman at Sears who told me that since working there she has had a decreased ability to think or exert any responsibility. Now, instead of looking at the price of an item and ringing it up on the cash register, she merely has to wave a magic wand over the tag and the appropriate numbers appear on the glass in front of her, thanks to the miracle of the computer. This eliminates possibilities of human error from the point of view of the employer but it also eliminates opportunities to utilize full human potential from the point of view of the *Daughter* role. The Sears saleswoman informed me that since she is given no chance to actively apply her mind to solve problems or think creatively on the job, she is very slow to do so at or outside work. This then is an impingement on her by her employer which has caused her great pain, sorrow, and feelings of worthlessness, humiliation, self-doubt and shame.

If the occupant of the *Daughter* slot tries to think or exercise judgment at work, she or he is likely to be dis-couraged from doing so or to be released from the position.

A blond blue-eyed boy hired
to sell specialty pastry un-·
derneath Grand Central Station at Christmas time epitomizes the structurally perpe-·
tuated ignorance of the *Daugh-·
ter* as compared to the *Fa-·
ther* in relation to work. "Quar-
ter pound of rugalach," I
said to him when passing
through one night. "What's
that?" Surprised, I pointed
to the pastry he was selling
which he had never heard of.
"Oh." "How much is it?" "I
don't know, I'll have to weigh
it." I said to him, "Could you

Hired for 2-3 days to shut
down a Nobils shoe outlet
in a shopping center in the
midwest, I experienced this
phenomenon. I observed
the process that I was supposed to do and said after
a few minutes that it made
more sense to organize
things another way. I was
told paternalistically,
"Sweetheart, Mr. Davis
has been shutting down
stores for Nobils across
the state. He knows what
he's doing. He's been do-
ing it for a long time." Be
that as it may, the revered
Mr. D. had been organizing the process from a short-
sighted perspective. As a newcomer I had an over-
view and could see that additional steps were being
required in the process of getting the shoes from the back,
off the racks and into the boxes. Nevertheless Mr. D.'s
time and greater experience, e.g., stability, was used as a
mechanism to silence me and to communicate that I
shouldn't be thinking. Both my immediate two-day bosses
preferred to get the right kind of coffee with the correct
number of sugar cubes over advice from me. And, much as
the Sears check-out woman, I was discouraged about my
own process of thinking. Maybe they were right, maybe
the way I saw the world made no sense to anyone but me.
This is oppression, internalized self-doubt. Being in the
Daughter slot impinges on the actor in that position. It
becomes a vicious circle: *Daughter* fulfills the expectations of the slot. She gets the job, does it routinely and gets
out fast. Then the employer can say, "See, this is the only
kind of job girls are fit for."

The advantage Mr. D. had over me was characteristic
of the *Father's* relation to work: the stability of his position. That he expects to stay is a determining factor in the
relationship of both the tenured professor and the auto
worker who gets a long-term union contract (a case where
brotherhoods organize for and achieve a *Father*-like

characteristic).* Each certainly gets a contract in the respective areas of work specialization and an assigned workspace, although in other respects these two jobs do not appear similar.

Furthermore, the long-term relation to work of the workplace *Father* means that the person carves out or is given his own area of responsibility. Earlier I mentioned an office in which the open middle room had three desks arranged in a semi-

> tell me the unit price?" "Uh, no—" Five minutes later he was still trying to decipher the flashing red and green lights. He picked up the bag he had filled and shuffled around to speak to the cook in the back. He was taking such a long time to get the answer to his question that finally I said to another sales person, a woman, "Is he all right?" Finally she waited on me, and the whole time he could hardly raise his eyes for fear he might have to look me in the face. This is the exact opposite, both for customer and worker, of an exchange in a *Father*-run store.

circle. I also said that around the center area each member of the professional staff had his or her own private office. Within their private rooms, professional staff conducted their work for an overall area of responsibility. The office as a whole did anti-corporate research and action. One person ran the agribusiness program, another the energy program, another the minorities activity. These separately-assigned areas are what I mean by the workplace *Father's* "own area of responsibility." And naturally, he who takes charge of one must think about the work and appropriately determine some portion of the workplace activity—as Mr. D. in the shoe chain did over me. In the shoe store other *Fathers* took other areas: getting boxes to trucks; filling out and filing forms or coordinating that procedure. When each of these shoe store *Fathers* had a task to be done in his area, he

---

*In this particular instance we can see how this is the reverse in the black family built on the mother and her kin network having the woman stable in the household and the various fathers and men going in and out. Not to promote the image of the no good black man but due to lack of stability in the family caused by racial discrimination and economic conditions this phenomenon occurs. For more see *All Our Kin: Strategy for Survival in a Black Community* Carol Stack, Harper Colophon Books, San Francisco, 1975.

called out to one of the other hired-on *Daughters*; when each of us finished that task, another *Father* could call out and claim our labor time. Our work changed while each of us stuck with our own area of responsibility. Likewise, a truck driver who has his own permanent cab often has his own route, his own area of responsibility, his territory. A writer for a magazine might be assigned to a special topic and achieve expertise there. The part-time secretary or research assistant only types the manuscripts given to her, and that somewhat randomly. Thus in terms of the relation to work, the job of the *Father* is characterized by stability with the congruent factor of his having his own area of responsibility. The latter both leads to and requires a different daily attitude about actually working: one that carries a concern or responsibility for what's going on at work.

The *Father's* relation to work is also characterized by finality, putting the pieces together, closure. This relation to work can be recognized in many situations: the doctor completes the operation, the L.P.N. merely preps for it; some auto workers put all the pieces together on the car while others repeatedly produce one accessory after another; the shopper for a restaurant buys the inputs, the cook has the pleasure of making the final soup.

A *Brother's* relation to work is characterized a bit differently because he expects to rise within the workplace structure. Thus when *Brother* enters the workplace he expects to maintain employment there for a number of years. And if he doesn't stay there, he will negotiate himself a better position somewhere else a bit further up the ladder in the same line, occupation, profession or industry.

A good depiction of this distinctive nature of the *Brother's* relationshop to work is that which transpires in the bull pen of the Madison Avenue advertising agency. Once a month someone enters the bull pen from the creative department. The representative offers the young drawers and inkers the opportunity to compete in coming up with a winning design for a particular product and customer. If someone does come up with a good concept, those in the creative department will reward the winner by using it.

What this ritual contest means in terms of the *Broth-*

er's relationship to work is that he holds expectations of being promoted in reward for performance. If he wins the contest often enough, he foresees the possibility of being transferred to the creative department. This forseeable future gives the *Brother* inker an attitude towards work clearly distinguishable from that of the Kelly Girl, hired to type for one day, as well as from the "girl" hired there permanently.

The *Brother's* future can be further foreseen in that he holds the power to go elsewhere and negotiate a position higher up in the hierarchy of another company. Showing his portfolio, he shows how his concept was used to advertise a product of an important client with the previous agency. He thus has the chance of being hired directly into the creative department on his second job, by-passing the bull pen completely. Thus a *Brother* can move up the ladder every time he changes jobs, whereas the *Daughter* cannot.

Of course, benefits such as these are only reaped if the *Brother* opts to stay in his chosen field of specialization. An intern in medicine cannot expect to get a good job in a law firm. Thus the *Brother* might also be said to suffer from "locked-in, nose-to-the-grindstone" oppression, part of the proletarianization of the professions. It should also be noted that not all incoming "first step" jobs are that good. Some don't even offer the appearance of permanency within the structure. An adjunct line at Brooklyn College may only be one semester; yet teaching one semester may mean Queens will offer a full line.

The *Wife* has a relationship to work which I call metaphorically "small parts." I got this metaphor from the auto industry. In Detroit, men are more likely to be employed in the lines of the Big Three industry. These big factories are unionized and offer substantial benefits to the workers: job security, high wages, health coverage. Wives of these auto workers, on the other hand, are more likely to be employed in the competitive factories making small parts—mirrors, accessories. These are sold by the small manufacturers to the Big Three where they are actually attached by the line workers to the final products of their cars. These men have long-term contracts and a commitment to engage over time in the basic automobile construction, while a mirror company might get shut down at a moment's notice with the passion of passing fashion. The *Wives* thus have a "dependent" relation to production.

The making of small parts is literal. But the small parts concept operates on an aggregate level as well. In the educational industry, the kindergarten or grade school teacher raises the child to a certain level of operational facility. In teaching discipline, reading, and other topics, she prepares the child who will later be "finished" by graduate school professors who take this small brain and turn it into that of a scientist, doctor, or lawyer. Thus in the "small parts" job, the *Wife* lays the basis for someone else's task completion. Or, after somebody else's task is complete, she does the maintenance work and "cleans up."* The task is still accessory, secondary, and furthest removed from actual involvement in production. This removal imparts the distinctive nature of the *Wife's* relation to work, that which makes the following people hold jobs which are all similar to each other:

> the woman worker in the Brooklyn silkscreening plant who hangs up the material after it has been designed and imprinted by others elsewhere in the plant;

> the cashier in the Latin American gold cage who takes the money after the butchers have sold the meat;

> the cleaning woman who sweeps up and empties the trash at night in an office after other people have worked in the day and made a mess of it;

> the secretary who has to make a neat and comprehensible letter on paper out of someone else's loosely dictated thoughts.

---

*For more clarity on *Wife's* relation to work as dependency, small parts, accessory production see some entries in Part IV. Here the workplace *Wife* (Norma Desmond's butler) dresses the actors but doesn't star in the movies. Or in the garment factory in which labels were sewn on coats flown in from Europe. The entire plant was in a *Wife* small parts role in relation to the aggregate structure of production centered elsewhere. Other notes explore aggregate and historical implications during the Industrial Revolution and in the Third World, which could also be expanded to encompass relations between center and periphery.

12.
RELATION TO OTHER WORKERS.

The workplace *Daughter*, not holding expectations to rise within the workplace structure, is less competitive with those around her in work performance. The *Daughter's* entrance into the workplace on a short term basis puts her in a situation

Box 5: Conditioned Daughter Docility

In the bank one day I asked the teller why two signatures were needed on withdrawals from savings accounts. "A precaution, I guess," she answered and then sighed to me, "After a while you don't ask why."

of docilely receiving commands, thus giving her a subservient relation to other workers with more experience and expertise accumulated over a greater period of time of working there. Performing her task by rote, over and over, she experiences less need for active cooperative relations to other workers. Stamp licking does not require "team work" the way coordination of joint projects or assembly like production does (see Box 5).

My job in the camera store selling film illustrates the qualities of a *Daughter's* relationship to other workers described above. I sold film behind one counter, and the camera salesmen stood across from me. They used to talk "sales talk" with each other. When a customer came in to empty the film from the camera, I merely labeled it and coded it, silently. But when a customer came in to purchase a new piece of equipment, all the salesmen had to talk, to pool knowledge, to give the best service to the customer, and try to win the sale and thus the commission. This dynamic drew the salesmen into a daily work-related interaction. Meanwhile, at any point in time I could be given a command which would whisk me from the premises. I could be sent off to the post office by the bookkeeper, or banished to the basement to print signs advertising sales to be conducted by the salesmen. As a "film girl," constantly interrupted by orders of bosses, other workers and even customers, I was estranged from the rest of the workforce rather than drawn in to cooperate or compete among them. This estrangement is typical of the *Daughter's* relation to other workers.

The workplace *Father*, on the other hand, has a qualitatively different relationship to other workers. Obviously, one factor is that he gives rather than takes orders. But this being in a position of determining work for others can happen directly or indirectly. For example, in the silk-screen factory we visited, the designer made the design which was executed by other people. He didn't necessarily have to be walking around saying "now you do this," "now you do that" to get the task done because the structure of everyone's tasks was organized around his designing decisions. Thus the pace of the *Father's* work generates both the pace and the structure of work for others, often with someone in the *Wife* role organizing such fulfillment.

That the work performed by the *Father* generates and determines work for others is true in particular workplaces as well as across the larger economic structure. The number of cars produced determines the number of mirrors, not the other way around. The number of cameras bought and sold determines how the bookkeeper should keep her books; the way she keeps her books does not determine the stock bought and sold in a camera store. The quality of food in a Greek restaurant determines the number of waitresses, and so on. In hundreds of ways, visible in daily interactions or not, the work of the *Father* determines the work of others; and this factor is crucial in defining his relation to them.

The *Brother's* relationship to other workers is defined primarily by competition. He believes that, in reward for work performance, he will have the ability not only to stay within the workplace structure but to move up. At the same time, he knows that not every *Brother* in his position in the workplace will be able to fulfill those expectations. Thus he will do what he can to make sure that he rises higher and more quickly than the others. Or even instead of them. Think about the bull pen in the Madison Avenue agency. Not every *Brother* inker will win that monthly competition. And not every *Brother* who wins will be promoted as a result. Thus the primary relation among workers in that bull pen is one of competition. Each *Brother* along one side of a counter selling equipment in a camera store will try to outdo the other for the loyalty of a customer. Of the three males tending the Brooklyn textile machinery, one may be promoted to foreman, but not all of them.

And finally, the *Wife* has a relationship to other workers in which she is disciplining them to follow the rules of the establishment, rules which are not her own. This she is often able to do from her vantage point of separated and isolated space, where she is held aloof and apart from the other workers. The best example I know is a story recently told me in an "economic consciousness raising" situation where I laid out the paradigm and invited a group of people to describe their jobs. In an informal workshop of women at the University of Michigan, a woman told me how she had once worked in an amusement park as a cashier. She was placed in a little glass box at the end of a row of workers who were selling refreshments. She was also asked, as part of her job, to watch over the other workers to be sure that they didn't steal the food they were selling. In another economic consciousness raising situation, a woman told me how she had once gotten a job in a Hartford insurance company. When she was hired, the older woman in the office instructed her in proper work attire. The other woman was enforcing the rules of the environment on the younger woman, a would-be sister worker. You can see how being in this situation creates hostility between other workers (*Daughters*) and the *Wife*, the enforcer—even though the *Wife* is not responsible for rule creation. The rules have been designed by the manager, the *Father*, the owner.

This role of the *Wife* in disciplining the other workers too can be seen in a larger aggregate structure, in two ways. One is that the entire job category of "personnel management" seems to be women in corporate management. This is the lowest level of management, the level on which no major decisions are made, the level at which workers are disciplined not to break rules and to shape up their behavior. The second is the way in which lower levels of management in a large corporation who appear to be *Fathers* in the immediate workplace are really only instructing their own workers to follow clearly-defined

> **Box 6:** Wife Enforces Father's Rules: Preparing For Others
> Task Completion
>
> At the District Center for Public Health, we shuffled in to get vaccinated. The *Wife* told us "pick up your boots, roll up your sleeves, walk by with the left arm facing the doctor, ask no questions." We'd walk by. The doctor would give us each a shot, one by one. We'd leave.

company rules. The assistant manager in an outlet of a McDonalds chain, for example, doesn't determine the work of those he employs, but only carries out the franchised package.* The same is true in the grade school classroom where the teacher is *Wife* to the Board of Education and to those who design the curriculum.

The interaction among other workers to ensure that the *Father's* role works right is often summarized as the Boss's Secretary Syndrome. She feels greater loyalty to her boss than she does to her objects, the other workers. The *Wife* is not just a discipliner, there is encouragement as well which she must perform. Often too she is doing the job for which the *Father*, being the figurehead, will claim credit. She has the responsibility but not the authority of the *Father*—a nurse must give injections but cannot prescribe the medication. As Doris Lessing points out, the Office *Wife* is often the "Office Mother," the helpful admirer under the structural authority of the *Father/ Child*. Thus the *Wife* identifies with the boss, acting like a mother in relation to *Daughter* and other workers, and women in that role participate in creating hierarchies among themselves.

13.
ON THE REWARD SIDE, with these four kin categories we see how workers in different slots are thrust into the family for survival reasons and non-material rewards (status, fulfillment, psychological reward and identification). And we see why some workers have greater hope for love and fulfillment in the domestic sphere, outside the workplace; and others have familial needs fulfilled in the workplace structure itself. Let's take the simplest material reward first.

The *Daughter's* economic benefits are few, obviously. The *Daughter* is not paid enough to support herself or to

---

*See Part IV where a class identified this assistant manager position as that of a *Brother* on the assumption that the *Brother* might become the *Father,* e.g., move up, and other plausible reasons. In present relations rather than projected future alignments, however, this low level management job could also be classified as *Wife*.

support others. The assumed reason is this: supposedly she is an economic daughter to a larger family where there are other wage earners. If she is earning anything, it is to "help out" around the house; or, to finance her first forays into freedom. This economic daughterhood is apparent at all stages of economic history. The first factory workers in America were young women who left farming households to come to the industrial areas. The same thing happened in China at the turn of the century. Not paid sufficiently for self-support, they lived in dormitories and saved and then returned home to the family. Even now, *Daughters* in the workplace are not expected to have to pay to keep a roof over their heads themselves. Since the *Daughter* does not earn enough to support herself, let alone to support others, she is forced to consider becoming a *Wife* in order to survive in the economic structure. She might also adopt the attitude that if she can't earn enough to support herself, maybe she shouldn't work at all.

Exactly opposite, as you might surmise, is the material reward of the economic *Father*. He is paid enough to support himself and his dependents. Trade unionists have often fought for higher wages for the male worker to support dependents on the grounds that after all he is a "family man." The economic *Father* also frequently works for some material incentive—as in the camera shop I mentioned, where the salesmen worked for a commission. They made a percentage—above salary—for selling camera equipment, whereas I could not earn more in my *Daughter's* job if I worked hard to sell film.

Not only does *Father* earn more if he works harder but he earns more if the people below him in the hierarchy work harder as well. Thus *everyone* works hard to improve *his* salary. This is true, for example, of the unit manager in an insurance company sales force.*

Because he earns more if he works harder or more frequently, *Father* will take overtime or work after hours while the less-rewarded *Daughter* probably will not.

In addition to monetary income, *Father's* job often

_____

*See Part IV for more discussion of the insurance industry.

has perks with it. The president of Brooklyn College gets a house; a car salesman gets his own personal use of the latest model. An executive traveling in the course of work gets an expense account. However, a secretary pays her own carfare or auto maintenance, along with lunches, even though percentage-wise this expenditure might represent a bigger proportion of her salary than the expense account does of his. Beyond the perks there are benefits: health plans, dental coverage, especially necessary for his "dependents." Because of the temporary nature of her work, these plans come less frequently with the *Daughter's* available employment.

The *Brother* is paid enough wages to support himself and expects in the future to be able to support others. This means he is paid more than *Daughter* and less than *Father*.

Finally, the *Wife* is expected to be primarily supported by others. Although the *Daughter* is assumed to be contributing to her paternal household, or living in a slip-shod way to reduce expenses (in a boarding house, dormitory, shared apartment, shacking up), the *Wife* is assumed to be pooling income with a husband. Or, it is assumed she is working to "fill in" with the rising expenses of raising children.

These economic discrepancies among the four different kinds of workers mean that at a certain point young women start looking for an economic out—pooling resources with someone of the opposite sex. This is especially so if a young woman decides she wants to have children. These economic discrepancies also pressure the Wife to stay within the marital structure, not out of love but rather out of economic necessity.

The discrepancies in terms of psychological reward in the various categories have the same effect. Neither *Daughter* nor *Wife* have very fulfilling work roles. Domesticity becomes the outlet. Women seek in the home what men get at work. By examining the characteristics we have stated so far, this statement can be grasped more specifically.

First of all, the kind of reward available to the workplace *Daughter* is peculiar. She can enjoy her docile subservient relationship. She can get pleasure from carrying out her acts with obedience. She can take a certain pride in not leaving a trace of herself, of being inconspicuous. She can enjoy the challenge of removing herself so far from the task that in no way can she be considered a bother. This is the good girl approach in which she might enjoy the self-abnegation of "fitting in." Alternatively, she might enjoy the intense fantasy life that comes from having to entertain yourself while keeping up appearances, as did the women faking accents in the credit department discussed as *Daughter's* subtle form of resistance in relation to work. In this sense *Daughter* gets the enjoyment of seeing how much she can get away with—the pleasure of out-foxing, the pleasure of tricking. This kind of pleasure borders on the pleasure of being disruptive and provocative. Where does the pleasure lie? In possibly provoking punishment. Another woman told me how she enjoyed the challenge of trying to get her boss to fire her. Her game went on for months: certainly more rewarding and challenging than taking the mundane work seriously. There is also the possible fantasy of seduction: the fantasy that the sexual power of the *Daughter* could stop workplace production. Or the fantasy of the power of gossip: *if* she were to sleep with the boss, she would have the power to tell. Especially because in the *Daughter's* head, the workplace *Father* is symbolically more her father than the boss she might enjoy pleasing.

I say the rewards to *Daughter* are peculiar because obviously these psychological rewards require a denial of self, a distortion of one's being for the sake of what? The rewards are shortlived in the sense that a real person in a *Daughter's* role ages and tires of approaching life like a game, especially as one begins to desire to live life more as oneself at the same time as one recognizes the degrees of alienation one must accept. As *Daughter* goes through these realizations, she adopts the depressed character structure of the *Wife*: accepting her lot with resignation.

Consider the opposite, the psychological rewards of

the *Father*. The *Father* more often commands status in the outer society. Not only does he have power over others, not only does he have greater fulfillment in his work being closer to or in control of his own task completion, but he enjoys respect for what he does. Since he has workplace stability, he enjoys the feeling of being wanted for himself, for what he can do, his connections and achievements. The only thing *Daughter* can offer as she looks for work is her ability to vacate herself. And she, unlike the *Father*, engages in the search endlessly. The *Father* can develop and carry greater security within himself. Wherever he goes he has a workplace identity which follows or even precedes him; whereas when *Daughter* goes to work, her identity is forced from her.

I hear protests already that the *Father* I am describing is an executive and not a working class father. Yet even a whisker-painter in a Brooklyn stuffed animal factory puts a little bit more of himself into his work and gets a little more satisfaction from it. And the truck driver gets the pleasure of making a place for himself when he decorates his private space with the girlie pictures. The exact opposite is true of the *Daughter* who, if she gets any pleasure at all, must get it from making herself inconspicuous. Furthermore, when teaching a night class in a working class community in New Jersey, I noticed how, as the men in working class *Father* jobs spoke, each of their stories took up an entire class section: a line man was a line man; a truck driver was a truck driver; and each had a lot to say about the importance of their roles to the phone company or the firm. And respect and interest from the class was there for them. We all listened and asked questions as these men with important interesting jobs spoke. I say this because of the job type, and not just because of the gender of the speaker. When working class men in *Daughter* roles (such as temporary help, grocery store checker) as well as women spoke, the stories did not merit such attention. In fact, those testifying to such position could only talk dispiritedly of how they had been ripped off, humiliated, and treated badly.

The *Brother's* rewards from work lies in the pleasure of winning the competition. Even if he leaves one job because he wasn't promoted and moves only one small rung elsewhere, he gets the pleasure of climbing. Each job *Brother* holds is in some small way an advancement over his previous employment. This is not true of *Daughter* or *Wife* jobs as they are both apt to experience disjuncture. The *Brother's* reward is also the camaraderie of competition even if he loses. He gets the reward of feeling he has made an impression, of feeling "they noticed me." And, as the advertising illustrator expects, he gets the reward of being promoted for good performance. We can see how this treatment grooms the *Brother* to become like the *Father*, while the *Daughter* nearly always drops out of workplace life and rewarded public existence.

What about the workplace *Wife*? Remember that all *Wives* were once *Daughters*. *Daughter* leaves the workplace to set up in domestic life what she observed and desired for herself in the day-to-day role of the *Father* at work. In the creation of the home, she seeks power by being the one to determine the tasks and structure. There she seeks to have her own area of responsibility. There she seeks security, stability, and a social role with widespread approval and recognition. There she seeks the power of determining the rules for others and of being the primary producer (of children and meals) rather than the accessory (money is the means to build a home, not the primary accomplishment). Eventually she is pushed back into the workplace, often out of disillusionment. She comes back to work (as *Wife*) ready to make do, not with the high expectations she had as a *Daughter*/explorer, conqueror, adventurer. She must get her pleasure from her ability to accomodate and compromise without experiencing the complete self-abnegation she felt when a *Daughter*. She gets the reward of making over others, of predicting the somewhat gloomy future. If she gets any source of power at all it is often in falsely identifying with the powerful workplace *Father* to whom she is subservient as he is her employer.

Why do I say the *Wife* is pushed back into the workplace after disillusionment in building a family. The disillusionment is in some ways economic. The *Daughter* thinks she is choosing economic security yet, with the divorce rate and fall-off in alimony payments, she often is not. Even if the family she has opted to build stays together, often as not, it turns out that, given inflation, the workplace *Father's* real wage falls short of the ideal. Once a *Wife*, she is not completely supported by her husband. The disillusionment is also emotional. Her husband gets solidarity, camaraderie, familiarity, a sense of his own space and self-worth outside the family. His primary ties appear to be with workplace *Fathers* and *Brothers*, not with his real wife within the home. And his dependents become a bother and a distraction from work.

14.
SKILL. That the *Father's* emotional ties are with other workplace *Fathers* and *Brothers* is accentuated by the acquiring and exercising of skills. Before I discuss the skill-bonding situation of *Fathers*, let me contrast the situation with that of the workplace *Daughter*.

Daughter, often as not, is required to use heterosexual skills learned not in trade school or on the job but in the nuclear family: a strip teaser and a belly dancer are obvious examples. Yet the requirement of heterosexuality might be more subtle: being expected to sleep with someone to get a job, to keep a job or to sell one's material. Or consider the aspects of heterosexuality required of a receptionist. She must dress nicely, flirt and be attractive to men as part of her boss's scenery. A waitress, too, must please. This is using the skills of the sex role, in that women are supposed to please men.

Besides applying aspects of sexuality, *Daughter* jobs consist basically of unskilled work. The skills of *Father* jobs, on the other hand, accumulate over the years. Their skills, knowledge and expertise must expand continually to keep up with the latest professional practices, the newest soap to sell, the newest machinery. Mechanics are periodically sent to General Motors schools by the dealers who sell those cars. Civil engineers for the city are required to keep expanding their number of licenses. Doctors take additional boards frequently. Economics professors have national meetings which they must attend to continue to teach and research properly; department secretaries don't. Thus, in many types of jobs, the meta-workplace functions can be identified as a *Father's* job characteristic.

Perhaps more significantly, both the accumulation and application of those skills serve the function of tying workplace *Fathers* together in interlocking networks beyond the individual workplace situation. This factor allows for the development of the feeling of "having gone through something together," often attained by initial rituals of indoctrination, periodic retraining, regrouping for weekends, lectures, conventions and conferences. These

Box 7: Interlocking Networks—How to Become a Father

Father's job also includes an understanding of how it all works, as illustrated in this "Honeymooners" story. Ralph wants to get a promotion to assistant traffic manager. The lunchroom rumors are quelled by someone saying "Mr Harper doesn't even know you're alive." Ralph tell his buddy, "It's not what you know but who you know. You won't get anywhere without connections." So he tells his buddy he'll start up a conversation with Mr. Harper.

His buddy says, "You tell him you're smart but you got no connections."

"No, I've been reading a book on how to influence people. I won't ask him about me, I'll ask about him. How's your daughter, I'll say, how's your wife? How's your son-in-law? Then when the promotion comes along, who do you think will get the job?"

"His son-in-law."

events bind those in *Father* jobs the way those in *Daughter* or *Wife* jobs might be bonded outside the workplace. That is, in the family. Additionally the sense of ties with others who are not part of one's day-to-day reality are increased through trade unions and professional associations the way family reunions, weddings and funerals serve to strengthen the sense of the individual's membership in a larger extended family. In both family and workplace *Father* functions, the individual goes away from the day-to-day situation and comes back feeling part of a larger unit of social organization, a deeply interconnected transcendant entity. The group experience is usually intense. In either case, one returns to one's family life or workplace infused with knowledge of oneself that was

Box 8: Daughter-
to-Wife Punt

A woman in service to the phone company for 40 years started as a long distance operator. Then she was sent to help in the office because she knew shorthand and typing. She finally "graduated" to work in personnel. The change in work situation paralleled changes in her life. When she first had her long distance service job, her hours were irregular, she was on call 24 hours a day, 7 days a week. She'd only work 40 hours a week, but she was never certain when. She married at 21 and had her first child at 24. At that point she needed the 9-5 regularity and changed to her job as a secretary. She was transferred to personnel the year before she retired.

just gained by the way one is seen by other significant persons: a grandfather, an aunt, a cousin, a niece or a son; a big shot in one's field, a graduate school advisor who invents the latest machinery, who can give you the finest most precise operating instructions, someone who organizes across the country to confront the bosses. One can be infused with a strength in these metafictions if the image of oneself reflected in those situations is good. That strength can lead to feelings of superiority which further separate *Fathers* from other workers when they return to their daily situations.

What is distinguishable about the *Brother* in his workplace skill is the training he gets right on the job. He expects to be given training when he signs up for work, and he usually receives this training from workplace *Fathers* who impart their skills, knowledge and expertise to him. For example, in the photography store mentioned in previous sections, the younger men across from me were learning from the older salesmen, informally. They would often learn after hours when they played basketball together, excluding me. Thus a person in a *Brother* job expects to learn skills, while a person in a *Daughter* job doesn't, or shouldn't.

Whereas the *Daughter* applies aspects of sexuality, the *Wife* applies the skills of homemaking and domesticity. Here the disjunction of *Wife* as utilizer of domestic skills versus the *Daughter's* use of sexual skills can be explained. The older woman is perceived as non-sexual by the patriarchal culture while the younger woman is perceived as sexual. The older woman also constructs herself as not sexual, identifying herself in relation to children rather than in relation to her husband or men. This follows her to the workplace, where she identifies herself according to her ability to discipline other workers as her children. Their following of the *(Father's)* rules she takes to be a reflection of her. My aunt is a good example of this. She worked in a millinery firm in 1918. In descri-

Box 9: Wife's Domestic Skills In Use, Advertising and Phone Company

All advertising firms have a department called "traffic." There is an art department and department that attracts clientele and handles specific accounts. "Traffic" makes sure the two departments talk to each other. Traffic has a high percentage of— you guessed it—women. Traffic is also the name of women's work in the phone company.

bing her job as a bookkeeper, she would roll her eyes and tell how she would walk into the bank and return with the payroll to distribute to everyone. Listening to her describe the situation, I sensed how she felt when doing this task. She wasn't determining the amount but distributing the portions. It was as if she were personally feeding people. In another case, a wife I know works as a supplier in a publishing house. Her job is to order materials. Like the wife in the home, she gathers inputs (for the family: sheets and food) for the publisher: paper, dye, ink and glue. How the materials will be used (what the family members will do with the rest they get on the sheets and the consumed energy) is not determined by the wife in the home or by the publishing house *Wife*. Other obvious examples are: secretaries making and serving coffee, reserving airline tickets for their bosses and keeping track of the dates their bosses' children will be shipped to and visited at summer camp. Thus in numerous ways a person in a *Wife* job is performing personal functions, or functions analogous to the ones a housewife performs at home.

One last point about the skills of the workplace *Wife*: her skills are non-cumulative. While I sold film in the camera store I watched the *Brothers* learn from the *Fathers*. The bookkeeper used to work in a little room in the back. I didn't learn from her in a day-to-day way. Indeed, I rarely saw her. When I did, it was when she would emerge from the back to send me on an errand or to make sure we all signed our paychecks. As I didn't expect

55

Box 10: Wife-Daughter Relations Can Be There Although Sex of Occupants is "Aberrant"

Gay men often get, as do black men, *Daughter* jobs. I once worked in a fast-food restaurant in the World Trade Center where many men behind the counter serving food in *Daughter* jobs were gay; likewise the occupant of the *Wife* slot disciplining them was a man.

to rise to become a bookkeeper, she did not impart her skills to me. If I had come to work in the store, I would have been transferred to her position. There would have been no relation between my ability to handle the books. As such, the workplace *Wife* experiences a disjuncture in work, an interruption in her application of learned skills.

15.

APPLICATION IS RELEVANT now that we have defined the four categories and separated them along the axes of distinguishing characteristics: space, relation to work, relation to other workers and reward and skill. I am now going to focus on one workplace situation to tie together all the disparate but related threads.

The Pontiac Dealer. Researching the employment opportunities for women in Orange County, New York, a team of women conducted series of interviews with local employers. In visits to employers we asked questions which would reveal information designed beforehand with the use of the categories. Both by questioning and careful observation, we recognized specific traits which helped to graphically identify the workplace *Daughter*, *Father*, *Brother* and *Wife*.

A color snapshot of his baby daughter caught our eye as Mr. C. preceded us into his private office. He was a sturdy-looking man in his early 30s of Italian extraction. Gesturing that we should distribute ourselves on his imitation leather couches and chairs, he strode behind his desk, eased himself into his swivel chair, and picked up the phone which was blinking inconspicuously. As we listened to Mr. C. conduct his business, his eyes shifted over the oak paneling which encased the room until they came to rest on a handprinted block-lettered motto pinned to a bulletin board: some clever wording about writing down one's goals in order to accomplish them. It struck us that Mr. C. certainly felt at home, and why shouldn't he? Not only the private space of the office but the business was his as well. There he sat, no doubt negotiating a deal's satisfactory closure, about to be interviewed, safely tucked into his own secure territory. Assembled behind him were souvenirs from his favorite sports—beer mugs, posters, pin-ups of sport cars, hand printed wooden ducks.

Mr. C., the workplace *Father* who owns and runs the business, has 17 full-time permanent employees in his firm. When asked to describe his job, he grinned and replied, "every team needs a leader." Mr. C.'s remark aptly illustrates a crucial characteristic of the categoric workplace *Father*—that he holds a hierarchical position over other workers. Grouped directly under Mr. C. in his chain of command were four other workplace *Fathers*—the body shop manager, the service manager, the new car preparation manager and the parts manager. Each of these in turn headed up his own department. Consequently, they each had other people directly responsible to them—for example, the service manager had five technicians working for him; and they each exhibited *Father*-like characteristics. Each of several mechanics worked for one or another of these *Fathers*; and four salesmen were also employed. Needless to say, all these workers were men.

Notice how each of these *Fathers* is designated by separate areas of responsibility. Yet, for each *Father* to operate independently, as a group they must be connected to each other or joined somehow to accomplish a job. This chain-like quality which gives *Fathers* a sense of cohesion is what I mean when I say that their skills are *interlocking*. The service manager must have regular exchanges both with the *Father* in the body shop and the *Father* in parts if he wants to promise the in-coming customer a certain date for delivery of the car. This chain-like cohesion extends beyond the specific place of the individual *Father's* work. For example, while in Mr. C.'s shop that day, I inquired if my heater could be repaired on my foreign car. The shop manager referred me to another place of business up the street, better equipped to do the work. He told me to ask for Joey and to tell Joey that he had sent me. This seems perfectly natural, yet stop and think and you will see that this linkage across workspace is much more characteristic of a typically male-held occupation. It has not been built into any typing job that one typist must have good connections to the other typists in other parts of the industry or business. Likewise, the typist is more isolated in the daily routine of task execution.

In this respect the *Father's* job is usually more social, more public; yet at the same time he is more committed to keeping family or workplace secrets. *Father* is quite concerned with building his workplace's name and reputation. "You work for everybody," a man who runs his own business told me when I once asked him how it felt to work for himself. With this nature of the work refining this *Father's* daily perception, he is always on the look-out for further business contacts which often extend to and define his social settings. By contrast, the secretary usually leaves the office at 5 o'clock, thankful that the day is done. She is not searching for more papers to type in the evening when she's out for fun. The same building of connections drives policemen to attend policemen's picnics where they might make an impression on someone who can move them up or elsewhere in the force; and professionals organize national and international associations.

This brings us to a problem Mr. C. faced when he first opened his establishment. The first three or four years of running his Pontiac dealership, Mr. C. reported difficulties in persuading good mechanics to stay in his shop. A good man, representing the place of work in a social or craft or professional context can easily be bought off by competitive establishments who seek to tempt him with a better job. Since *Fathers* accumulate skills which make them indispensable, the employer often encourages competent knowledgable *Fathers* to stay around, putting together attractive packages. The *Father* might be paid not only in higher wages but also with privileges and benefit schemes. Our workplace *Father,* Mr. C., offers his salesmen and other key workers a new Pontiac each year to drive as a demonstration model but also to use on their own. They are also enticed to stay by a cumulative life insurance policy. Since any *Father* is aware of the market which exists for capable men, when accepting employment, the terms are often negotiable. "It's an open market," Mr. C.'s service manager says, "and you try to get a good deal when you come in, depending on how much experience you've had and on how much the dealer needs you." The range of ways to be paid is wide—by flat salary, incentives, piecework. The body shop manager we talked to identified himself as "paid by the clock," but he is also allowed to use the shop to take jobs of his own on the side. The body manager fills this shop with his own tools, representing the accumulation of a $3000 to $4000 investment. Although the reason for this arrangement was difficult to discover, one of the women on our interviewing team knew from an auto mechanics course taken in a vocational school that mechanics and others working in auto shops are known to take tools with them when they go on to a better deal with another employer or when they go into business on their own. Consequently, she later explained, Mr. C. and most dealers require men working for them to purchase and use their own equipment. Mr. C. thus saves himself from making outlays for capital investment and, at the same time, enhances the sense of a personalized working space held by the workplace *Father* on the job.

On the issue of space, let's have a look at Mr. C.'s floor plan. His office (see below) has the most privacy. In the back on the right-hand side. Mr. C.'s office also has a window. Each of the salesmen has his own semi-private space, partitioned on the right hand side of the show room by the low walls. The two desks of the bookkeepers have been stuck into a smaller, completely shut-in windowless area, showing how the *Wife* frequently works separated and isolated from other workers. Women are also boxed in separately, a salesman explained, so they won't "distract." This typifies the assumption of the mandatory sexuality in the *Daughter's* job. As one of the salesmen put it, "if you have attractive women working in the place,

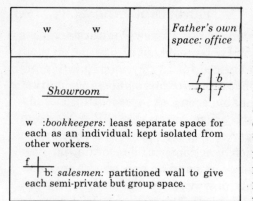

w :*bookkeepers:* least separate space for each as an individual: kept isolated from other workers.

b: *salesmen:* partitioned wall to give each semi-private but group space.

it would be a distraction for the guys working." Such a reason was also given for not hiring women to sell cars, a more lucrative occupation than bookkeeping or filing in the auto business. The hired women would invade the physical "group" territory of the men. And, as Mr. C. himself expressed, if he hired a woman to sell, he would stand to lose some sales, as wives would get jealous of interactions between female sellers and husbands when married couples would come to shop for cars.

The two bookkeepers, on the upper left hand side, ran a "two girl office," as one of them said. The bookkeepers were both women in their sixties. Although we had come to have a tour of the entire business, we were not ushered into the women's office nor given the opportunity to learn very much about their jobs. We might have expected this, as it is not often the responsibility of the *Wife* to represent the firm to the public. Her job is more domestic in that she takes care of business on the inside. Even after we requested a chance to speak to the women, Mr. C. did not choose to personally introduce us, thus signalling the two women that it was all right to stop for a moment to talk. Yet he extended this authoritarian courtesy to the other working people, men only too eager to have a chance to discuss their jobs. When we did enter the "two-girl office" on our own they were too busy preparing reports for the auditor to take a few minutes off. Mr. C. had already informed us that he employed three women. In addition to the two elderly bookkeepers (*Wives*) there was also a 25-year old filing "girl." She was not in sight and by the bookkeepers' description of their workspace as a "two-girl office" she revealed this younger woman (obviously a workspace *Daughter*) to be as invisible to the two bookkeepers as they had been to Mr. C. A discerning *Daughter*-like characteristic: disappearing anonymously into anonymous work. No wonder *Daughter* never established a continuous on-the-job presence.

By contrast, we interviewed the young man employed to run the body shop. He occupied the back third of Mr. C.'s shop, separated from the main garage by walls and doors. There he is rarely invaded by the casual passing of customers. This gives him freedom to decorate his over-sized room with posters of nude women advertising various automotive finishing products. "Finishes you can stand behind," boasted the lettering along the bottom of one vivid poster. Above were four pairs of coquettishly pointed toes, four sets of calves, four sets of thighs, four bright shields of different tones of paint, four pairs of breasts just barely covered by the shields at the nipples, and then the smiling heads of the four naked impish women. The body shop manager not only showed us how having a personal space in which to work allows *Fathers* to create an environment which they really take as their own but he also illustrated another *Father*-like characteristic: his ability to derive more satisfaction from his job and his greater likelihood of seeing the results of his labor. As he gloated when asked to describe his job, "It's like sculpture, an art—when you are all done you can look at your work, and others will admire it."

When asked where he got his experience, the young body shop man explained, "Back in 1960 when my father sprayed his car in the driveway!" This typifies how *Brothers* learn from *Fathers*, whereas *Daughters* seldom learn workplace skills from *Fathers* or *Wives*. Workplace *Brothers* not only learn from *Fathers*, they also take from *Fathers* in order to rise. This, as we saw, led Mr. C. and others like him to require that in-coming mechanics be hired with their own tools. This of course creates another handicap for women.

The body shop man exhibited an exaggerated disdain for what can be learned through formal educational channels. He spoke of the nearby trade school which offered courses on auto mechanics with contempt. "That's where you go instead of reform school," he scoffed. "There you are taught by the book—but if you go into any big shop, you'll see they have one guy who is smart, learned on his own..." A problem created for women here is that often vocational school is the only channel open for women seeking entrance into this line of work. "But the only way to do it is to apprentice on the side," he insisted. When asked if he would be willing to take on a woman and instruct her, as his own father and workplace *Fathers* had done for him, he thought not. "Why, my wife would divorce me if I apprenticed a woman here, unless this place had glass walls."

Yet Mr. C. trains men who enter his establishment as potential risers or *Brothers* (who then protect their territory, as can be seen in the body shop man's remarks). For instance, Mr. C. currently sends an incoming mechanic to a special school run by General Motors to prepare people for the issuance of new equipment. And a 22-year old male salesperson was just hired, despite his apparent lack of knowledge about cars. M. C. himself is undertaking the young man's training. And the plate glass walls in the new car showroom have not enhanced a saleswoman's chance for equal opportunity. The starting salesman began at a salary of $75 a week, probably paying less than the filing job held by the workplace *Daughter* if she were to work full-time. But the *Brother* is also entitled to material incentives in the form of commissions he gets from selling cars. The new, eager salesman explained, "It's a 50-60 hour work week, 9-6 on Saturday, 9-9 four days a week. But the more hours I put in, although there is no increase in salary, I could get a bigger crack at landing a sizable commission."

Before leaving Mr. C.'s shop, he told us that he was willing to speculate about hiring a woman in something outside ordinary office work. He thought the service division would be a good place to bring women in, eventually; and the service manager agreed with him. The service manager himself was a man who "came up through the ranks," as he put it, a characteristic of a *Brother* who had fulfilled his expectations of rising to the top. He started off years ago as a mechanic and then went into business for himself. He owned and operated two Exxon stations each with a 24 hour towing service. He wanted to get out of business when the headaches got too great, whereupon he answered ads in the local newspaper. But having been a Big *Father* once and facing a future in which he might become one again, he identified with that Big *Father* feeling and still thinks like a businessman even while in his salaried job. He has been thinking of further subdividing the work in his department. He would create the position of service writer—someone who fills out forms while listening to the incoming customers' worries, problems and complaints; and that of floor manager to coordinate the department-to-department flow of the work. He himself would remain chief service manager. Needless to say, it's the service writer's paperwork job he is considering giving to a woman. After all, it would be dead-end, with no opportunity to rise because the head of the department would still need a working knowledge gained not by shuffling two dimensional papers but by handling three dimensional cars.

PART III

GROAN AND GRUNT FOR BED AND BOARD. YES VIRGINIA IT REALLY IS DADDY

16.
SOMETIME IN MY late 20s, I went to a rather fatherly type in a publishing house. An editor. I was job-seeking. I asked the man what I might expect as a salary. He told me, $125 a week. I protested. The reason I was seeking work was that my rent was going up to $400. If I took such a job, I could barely cover it. Well, the kindly editor informed me, it's a buyer's market. "Most of these girls still live at home. Or else, you know—they shack up. You say you want $10,000 a year on a part-time job? So you can keep writing? Well," his eyes dropped to my crossed knees, implying, "you know what you can do for that." I smiled pleasantly, if a bit bitterly, angrily thinking, "and this from a friendly sort who has read my first book and knows my track record."

That night I had dinner with an old friend, a guy a year younger than me whom I knew from college. College—those were the days, though I didn't think so then. He and I had seemed more equal at the time. We were both young, bright; full of ideas, ambition, creativity. I went into writing. He went into film. Over dinner I learned he had earned $25,000 that year and that he expected to make $35,000 the next. After dinner we went back to his sublet basement studio apartment. On his annual income of what it would take me five years to earn, he lived like a migrant, a packrat, a hobo. I held down a loft on what I made winging it—but I had come to a time in my life when

I wanted a tub that worked and furniture. I sat on his bed, musing over the discrepancies between needs, wants and capabilities. He was packing. He kept saying he had to go out of town on a shoot the next day, warning me not to get too comfortable for he was going to send me home. But shocked by the difference in our earning capacities and social status, stunned by the widening gap of relative power and powerlessness between us, reeling under the realizations of how men gain power as they grow older and women lose it, I persisted in forcing a personal conversation. Something which was never easy between us. Something which for the last ten years he has tried to avoid, and I have wanted to push, and we could both feel it.

"P—," I began, "when I saw you the last time, you said now that your career has come to a plateau you could turn your attention to other concerns—remember? In the kitchen?"

"Yep." Taciturnly.

"What did you mean?"

He packed silently for a few seconds.

Then he grunted, his back to me. "Nuclear energy?"

"What? Are you serious?" Because I had gone away with suspicions from that lone remark that P— was ready to get married and have children. That his remark about "other concerns" had been a hint, and that what he wanted was for me to pick up on it. "Do you want to know what I thought?"

"No."

I should have told him anyway. I had begun to spend my unemployed days wandering through the domestic floors of New York department stores fingering linens, pricing dishes and beds, imagining what kind of furniture we would buy, what kind of apartment, what kind of rugs. Instead of confessing my domestic fantasies, which I thought would be too much for him, I turned the conversation to the dormant sexuality between us. Here P— explained that for our history of ten years, he had always felt a great deal of care, concern and respect for me. He saw me as someone with a great deal of insight, whom he admired but not as someone he was attracted to sexually. I decided to get him to talk about his sexuality so at least I could know what, for P—, this was. Then I'd figure out what he wanted and how to maneuver it. His last great lay, I was told deliberately, had been when he was out of town on a shoot. I asked the obvious: what was so great about it. Well, they met, he hardly knew her. The passion was physical and the memory dissolved the next day as he returned to the shoot and his mind fell back to daily activity. He made a gesture, while telling the story, of bending over and waving his hands behind him to show how as he began to concentrate on the work awaiting him on the shoot, the night behind him began to dissolve and he let it go at that. That had been his last thought of her. He looked pleased with himself, restful, wistful, as he concluded the story.

I cringed listening, at the difference between us which I saw as not only a difference between P— and myself but as a difference between men and women. My heart went out to the poor "lay" whom I surmised was probably still thinking about him if indeed, as P— described, the sex had been that good. While I watched P— pack for his job, I remembered the way the sex I had had the night before had been the only way I could survive my last $3.88/hour research job. If enough good sex from the night before could fill my mind, the details of the paper work and the staff meetings and the humiliating encounters with the coordinator would roll right off me. I could run my eyes half-heartedly over pages of statistics and not even feel it, remembering someone loving me. Wasn't that what sex was for? To act as a protective barrier between yourself and work? Between your mind and the impersonality of the statistics or facts or petty problems that might invade you? No, not if you are able to put yourself into work, the way men do. And men use their power and status at work to act as a protective barrier between themselves and women.

I "humpfed" loudly to myself at that, and just then P— looked up, announced that he was through packing, that it was time to call a cab, that I couldn't stay, or else he'd sleep on the floor fitfully—and after all, he had to go to work the next day...

17.

TO GET AT THE ROOT of the many scenes in women's lives, we must see how the family produces divided consciousness in workers in support of the material basis of sex and age divisions of labor. As might be surmised, the subjective experience came first, and the objective categories *D-F-B-W*, delineated in Part II, were generated by trying to understand the structure that created those feelings and to order the experience. A visualization might make things easier:

conscious	objective structure	division of labor etc.
unconscious	subjective experience	what makes people go on with it

What generates the subjective experience of the different consciousness of men and women at work? This is the question here, as we have already examined the objective parameters of the structure. Exploring the underlying subjective processes congruently at work does not discount the objective processes. Understanding the family, its dynamics, and its effects on our species allows us to see what propels people to keep participating in the *D-F-B-W* grid even though such participation is crippling to the human condition. In my view, it is not sufficient to answer "Why do people do it?" with the brief and simple "Because that's how it is."*

To understand what keeps the system cycling on and on, it is useful to spot and consider in depth what some

---

*Given women's day-to-day lives of performing boring, meaningless work for low pay, the "sensible" solution might be to do as the Arizona Indians did. At 16, young men could decide whether to kill themselves or not. If they chose to do so, it was an accepted act within their culture, not something which was labeled "sick."

have identified as the core of the problem which needs to be changed. Recent feminist-Freudians have suggested that what women need in terms of large scale social change is the abolishment of single-parent child care arrangements.* When all children are dependent on the primary care of a single female parent—the argument goes—a distorted consciousness is created.

Marxist writing for a long time has advocated that child care be taken out of the individual family and collectivized mostly because the woman is doing "double duty"—meaning that women (in their capacity as mothers and wives) have a double duty to perform, at home and at work, which keeps women at a disadvantage on entering the labor force even under socialist conditions. That is, they must shop, care for children, clean house, and cook; as well as perform the paid labor hours. This leaves them with less energy for their "primary responsibility" as child rearers and homemakers. And, of course, the years they are out of the labor force giving birth makes them undesirable material to the employer who wants full and unconditional access to the potential laborer. With this double duty crunch, Engels explained why the woman's participation in labor, which Marx thought would free her, does not. He, of course, didn't see how differences in sex and age did not disappear as each individual worker joined the pool of hopefully androgynous collective labor.

But here we have a further reason to advocate a society which breaks down single-parent child care arrangements. Such an arrangement creates a situation in which males are dependent on the female during early childhood, the psychological effect of which is that men's coming to adulthood, among other things, is a process of getting away from woman as a maternal, threatening symbol. If one gives credence to this theory, the reason men are more threatened than women by relations to women is that when completely vulnerable as an infant the little boy

---

*Nancy Chodorow, *The Reproduction of Mothering: Psychoanalysis and the Sociology of Gender,* University of California Press, Berkeley, 1978; Dorothy Dinnerstein, *The Mermaid and the Minotaur: Sexual Arrangements and the Human Malaise,* Harper Colophon Books, New York, 1977.

sees one who is different from himself on two counts: female and adult. On two counts the Mother is Other. For the little girl, the two counts are reduced to one: Mother is Adult; but Mother is like daughter, female. If it follows that men would be more threatened in relating to women, it would also follow that one small part of this consciousness is the consciousness carried to and acted out in the male-created arena of work.

Given the nuclear family and exclusively female-parenting arrangements (even if only in the first months or first years), the tenacity of men's belief in the world of work—the monster they have created—is a defense against that primary initial dependence on the female. Psychologically, work and the strong tenacity to which men as men hold on to it must be more than itself. Symbolically work must mean more than a means to an end of security and accumulation of possessions. Consider here work as an attempt to compensate for renunciation of infantile desires, the satisfaction of which is represented by the female, due to single-sex parenting at an early age. Thus participation in the world of work to men *as men* not just as survivors, earners, or even as people, is very important to them. Have you ever heard a working class man come home and lament to his woman that he is not being treated "LIKE A MAN" at work? How does that lament make her feel and what is the origin of it, and why does he—the working class man—want above all respect from his woman for it?

To take the logical step further, this belief in the world of work as an escape from women becomes a barrier to the development of class consciousness which Marx thought would emerge from the proletariat. Once in possession of this class consciousness, Marx thought, the proletariat could proceed to take over factories and create a class-made revolution, socializing the means of production and abolishing ownership of productive properties. Yet what we have seen is one barrier to the execution of this class revolution stemming from the underlying division of the male-centered work world and the female-centered child's world in the family. That is, the reason we don't have a socialist revolution against capitalism is because we live in a patriarchy. Specifically, a patriarchy in which men control work and women control childhood.

Still, this logical application of the mechanism discussed by the feminist-Freudians centers on male needs, male beliefs, and the effect *on men* of female-dominated early childhood. A reversal needs to be developed to locate the conditions which need to be changed to allow both the development of class consciousness and the liberation of women.

To understand the reversal, the mechanism is: a consciousness of themselves as a class does not develop among workers because of female-dominated early childhood, which makes going to work (for men) into an escape from the mother, the female. And to elaborate: once there, the controlling consciousness is not that they have become workers or managers, professionals or businessmen, truck drivers or pimps, but that they have become men. The need to cling to the world of work as a female-less refuge, the world of adulthood where helpless little boys have become big strong men, leads to the creation of barriers to females. These barriers include severe limitations on what jobs women are allowed to do. A woman can come to work but she has to act as a *Daughter*, be cute and flirtatious and sexy. A woman can work but at a low level job and she cannot expect to rise further. A woman can work but she won't be paid much or equally; a woman can work but only under the control of some man. A woman can work but she has to submit to sexual assaults. These barriers are created and enforced in tandem by all classes of men. Thus men, overcoming class divisions among themselves spontaneously, cooperate to push women back to the home, the family. Thus placed, the chastized female, chased from the world of work into domesticity, has no choice but *again* to dominate early childhood. The cycle reproduces patriarchy again.

Now, for the reversal. As Marxist theory focuses on the adult male, Freudian theory focuses on the little boy. I am going to shift the object of analysis to the little girl, asking: what effect does this division have on the little girl? What happens unconsciously as she sets out of the house as her brother does, trying to become an adult, only to discover that she must go back home and find her fulfillment being a woman? Or rather, to become dependent on a man as forced by material conditions? Specifically I will ask what effect do the material conditions of the wife's economic dependence on the male and the child's economic dependence on the father have on the little girl inside each attempted woman-as-worker? The ideal paradigm for this is the household in which the mother is economically dependent on the father, that is, fully responsible for the childcare and the housecare while the father works. Although statistically speaking this formation will not occur in all households at any one point in time, this is the type of structure adopted in the child's early years even if, prior to the child's birth and in the near future, the mother will again have some relation to work. This is all derived, as I have said, on the theory that the child's early years determine a lifetime of consciousness. Furthermore, this image is transmitted through cultural inputs to re-indoctrinate people if they don't get enough of it in early childhood.

So starting from that household: as going to work for men is done as an escape from the female, going to work for women is also a move to escape the mother, only that mother is a female like herself. Once at work, the controlling consciousness for men is that they have become men. Once at work, for females the controlling consciousness is that they have entered the world of the father—given the simultaneous existence of the structure of work and the nuclear family. Since the little girl still identifies with the female, going into the father's world without the mother whom she leaves in the home, is symbolically equated with the commission of incest in the unconscious. Incest is technically defined as sexual intercourse between persons too closely related to marry legally. By symbolic incest I mean the close relations with other family members that activate appropriate fantasies in the minds of the actors and even propel the actors in one direction or another in the hope of sexual-fantasy fruition. In the logic of the latter: all little girls want to "sleep" with their fathers, the first available sex object but they can't in the presence of their mothers. Therefore if they follow the father out of the house and enter his world symbolically in an attempt to differentiate themselves from the mother, they have done so simultaneously experiencing a desire to corner the father free of the mother, on his own territory, outside the confines of the mother-dominated house. Once at work, the consciousness of women is not that they have become adults, but that they are daddy's little girls.

To continue with the reversal and to psychologize the world of work from the daughter's head to understand her mode of consciousness within the framework of her existence there: the male raised in a mother-dominated house needs to cling to the world of work as a female-less refuge. This leads him to create and impose barriers against equal female access to that world. The little girl, on the other hand, needs to cling to the right to be out of the house far away from her mother—a right which is not as clear because of her fusion with the same-sex parent she leaves at home. To cling to her right to be out of the house in the face of the incestuous desire which has motivated her to be there, she accepts that world as sexual. This leads to her repetition of compulsive heterosexual behavior, the object being the men at work: co-workers, bosses, colleagues, directors, foremen, employers. Remember, because of the male need to erect barriers to her, the men are submitting the female who enters the workplace to sexual assaults which she responds to unconsciously as her only reason and right to be there. She also takes these assaults because symbolically the male at work is *Father*, her first object of sexual desire, and because she assumes these assaults are deserved punishment for her unconscious motivation to be there. She further accepts limitations on pay and type of work as punishment for the incestuous desire which brought her there. And, because she thinks that marriage will make this existence short term, she thinks she has a way out. But for her moment of being there, feeling unconsciously guilty for seeking her *Father* at the office or factory, she'll accept any bit part or humiliating conditions just to be there.

The world of work represents for men the world of adulthood where helpless little boys have become big strong men. This "becoming" is achieved with his mother's recognition, her bestowed awe of his achievements in a world which is beyond her comprehension. He has finally surpassed the mother on whom he was once so dependent. He can turn and dominate her and so he is at last free to dominate other women. Usually, until he has achieved a certain status in the world of work and his mother's recognition of his accomplishments, he is too threatened by woman-as-mother to do so.

The little girl, on the other hand, never overcomes her helplessness partly because her own real mother rarely overcomes her ambivalence about her daughter's work world achievement. Women who have become dependent on a male's earnings often resent their daughter's apparent freedom from such a relationship. This resentment in turn causes them to throw up obstacles to the daughter's achievement, even before withholding what the boy gets automatically—the mother's seal of approval. These obstacles vary with the situation but may take one of the following forms: threatened or actual denial of access to other things a daughter gets from a family when she obediently stays in the sex role; a jealously motivated over-protectiveness based on the mother's knowledge of the sexuality she knows her daughter is prey to; or claims to a large proportion of her *Daughter's* earnings. These punishments differ with varying positions in the class structure.

The daughter takes these reactions to her efforts at work achievement as punishment. She clings to the only recognition she gets: sexual recognition from men which has already dominated her experience at work. She decides to turn herself from a helpless little girl to a big strong woman, not in the world of work, but in the exercise of the illusory power of sexuality to arrive at its so-called epitome—domesticity with motherhood as the ultimate achievement. Having done so, she finally reaches adulthood, not as a powerful autonomous person, but as a tamed shrew. This sad and sorry, often resigned decision interlaces with the structural barriers facing her in the workplace (barriers erected by men, which might induce economic panic as her needs rise and she hits ceilings on her earnings), the overreaction of her mother, reactions of other reinforcers of patriarchal attitudes and institutions, and her own view that she deserves to be punished for going to work in the first place. This was, remember, unconsciously the illicit pursuit of the father. And this pursuit was the beginning of the exercise of her autonomy. Hence the exercise of autonomy, which makes a man proud, makes a woman feel shameful and guilty. This determines her relation to sexuality as a negative and degrading rather than autonomous force. When on top of that, due to barriers in the workplace, she finds herself thwarted, she tries to escape into domesticity in a chastized status, filled with a morose self-blame for it.

As to the effect of the family: men, having achieved at work and won their mother's recognition, are ready, as has been suggested, to dominate women in personal relations of their own choosing. Women, on the other hand, go through the reverse process and come to relations with men with their needs for affirmation of adulthood *ready to be fulfilled* eventually by the creation of family. But often as not, the man has already achieved adult status and he treats her like a child. He remains the adult and she becomes the child-partner. On the other hand, he wants her to continue his mother's now-recognized awe of his achievements. Since she has tried "out there" and lost, now feeling humiliated as well as shameful and guilty, she (not fully seeing or sensing the barriers erected to women which make things more difficult for her than for him) must give this recognition to him. She is by this time economically dependent, having achieved her adulthood by handing over the world of work to him, becoming his personal servant, and taking up maternity. Her daughter is raised with earliest visions of the mother at home and the father at work. The cycle begins again.

The basic conclusion is two-fold. First, if guilt for illicit pursuit of father defines the inner psychology of women-as-worker, the woman is not going to develop a consciousness of herself as a member of a class any quicker than the men who are humiliating her and degrading her in attempts to protect their female-less refuge at work. Rather, work is going to give the woman an increased consciousness of her sexuality and consciousness of the use of her sexuality to get out. Thus, while in Marxist analysis women's participation in the labor force was key to emancipation, we can see how participation in the labor force under the current structure might make women cling harder to the very familial arrangement which constitutes their oppression.

And secondly, while women have a track which they can try to "duck out" on, ostensibly to find extra-workplace fulfillment, men don't. Jealousy of this route available to women might make men cling harder to their desperate belief in the value of the world of work, its rightness, even in the face of obvious exploitation and corruption—which also constitutes clinging to their own (class) oppression. Thus the dream of a unified working class remains, at best, stillborn if indeed it has ever been created.

18.

THE QUESTION THEN BECOMES what structural economic change can be made to bring about a more humane working situation which allows women to seek power (economic and otherwise) with and for themselves rather than through a man as is currently required in the interlocking family and work systems? Or, what condition has to be changed in the current structure to terminate this circuitous process described in the previous section? We are already building on the assumption that early childhood dependence on the single family parent for mothering must be rearranged. In addition we will add the suggestion that economic dependence of children on fathers must be stopped. So, in answering the radical feminist question: what else needs to be done besides socializing the means of production to liberate women, we have arrived at an answer—the breaking down of income pooling across sex and age lines; the proposal (made in *Curious Courtship*) is to pool income within each sex and age group as a unit—a mini-state responsible for making its own decisions. We also propose the dissolution of the family which currently supports the sex and age division of labor in the patriarchal structure of work by reproducing the divided consciousness of workers.

19.

SO FAR WE have discussed incest as a controlling consciousness in *Daughter's* head from the angle of a concept in male derived Freudian theory. Freud had a concept of looking at psycho-history and the origin of social structures from the point of view of the son. I reversed that, or switched it over to the *Daughter's* perspective, but I was still using an inversion of his theory. This move or method could be dismissed as a lot of gibberish, sort of like deriving the square root of negative one to try to get to the positive, instead of making up our own thought forms or generating our own number systems.

Many are making up new modes of consciousness, particularly in incest survivor support groups which are mushrooming all over the country. Part of the self-help movement's protest against traditional concepts and practices in therapy. Attending these groups, or listening to the women who explain the effect that experience has had on them provides a space to tap into the same flow which fed into the *Daughter's* consciousness described in the workplace dynamic section. So curiously enough even if we throw out the male thought forms altogether to look at the quality of consciousness created in the *Daughter* who has been an actual survivor of incest in the family, the result is similar.

PART IV

VARIATIONS ON SOME THEMES: FROM THEORETICAL OBSERVATION NOTEBOOKS INSTANCES OF THE SEXUAL POLITICAL ECONOMY

20.
WE NOW KNOW
something about
how the theory de-
veloped, the objective parameters of sex and age division of
labor at work and the kind of consciousness originating in
the nuclear family that keeps the whole thing going. We
have also suggested changes that might be made and
short of that how the consciousness created might itself
disrupt. These themes and variations vary that context
greatly, if not endlessly.

These notebooks are discursive not linear and so are
to be perused as photographic contact sheets. They were
kept at a time when I had this particular framework in my
mind and saw various aspects of it continuously. In writing them down I was re-ordering the previously unob-
served. I began to look for the patriarchal moment; to stop
the world in a moment of time to discover the crucial
relationship, as some of the boxes in the text have also
done. In these notebooks, the family roles or kin categories are the basic formulation which multiplied a number
of times produce the patriarchal structure of work. They
were kept to pin down an inchoate consciousness, initially
observed or envisioned as flashes and which first emerged
as takes in the head of a main character in a novel in
progress. Thus giving myself freedom in form, I allowed
myself to generate new content.

In photography I had learned to discover a place, to
go there, shoot, go home, and look at the contact sheets;
look again, print some, go back to shoot, look at the sheets,
go back and shoot, print again. This is how I began to use

my notebooks. I went to "shoot" or observe and write down observations and reflections in different ethnic groups, in different working class neighborhoods, in hotels in New York where out-of-towners would be attending occupational and professional conventions. Seeking out disparate situations, I would talk to and gather information from many kinds of people. I would be observing and listening for many qualities and characteristics. I saw theoretical reflections that I began to organize in a notebook called "Theoretical Observations." In the process of separating all these notebooks, I also began a separate journal of daily continuity and a separate journal for therapy. This way I controlled for what I realized at some stage of the game had been happening which is, that I would take an insight attained in therapy and see it reflected everywhere. I devised a notebook system in which I sorted out what insights to pursue on my own.

These insights I am presenting to you now are not necessarily arranged and ordered except as they were seen and felt. The philosophic books I had been reading on the structure of thought gave me the idea that the examples I was recording could be used as illustrations to suggest the contours of a new vision, not necessarily to prove the merits of its existence. The value of suggestion over definitive declaration became clear to me. The notebooks follow a trial and error process saying "this might be so, look at this, consider this fact this way" rather than proclaiming "this is it."

The notebooks are organized around clusters of observations: workplace observations, reinforcement institutions, class and race factors, implications of consciousness, and work, sexuality and money. Some entries are referred to a number of times or examined with different motives or intents. This is not repetition but acknowledgment that, examined from different viewpoints, each observed relation might have different meanings and consequences. That is what the *process* of theory development is about.

21. Objective parameters: the grid at work

1. Some examples of space: The fashion designer with three women on each arm; not only his own space, but the liberty to transform the space of other people. Or the admitting room at Roosevelt Hospital. When I first went in, the man in the father-like job upstairs saying "I feel like Santa Claus" offered a deferment of payments. We were sitting in his private office. Then he took me downstairs to the *Wife*. She sat behind a desk, calling the names of the patients waiting in the public space. When my name was called, a *Brother* came out to the public space to meet me. He took me down the hall to the rows of cubicles and into a portion of the *Brothers'* group space. There he took my valuables for the safe deposit box. A *Daughter*, a volunteer candy striper, then came in to take me to another floor to finish being checked in. She was like a department store runner: free space or no space of her own to work in. The diagram of the space looks like this:

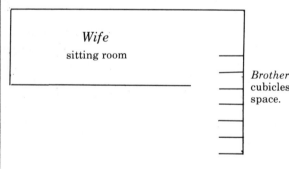

2. In the sociology department of a college in which I once taught, the department secretary had her own small room tucked into the corner of the hall. The research department, a separate room, had the desks of all the *Brother*-teachers. The space diagrammed looks like this, showing how the *Wife* is separate from other workers:

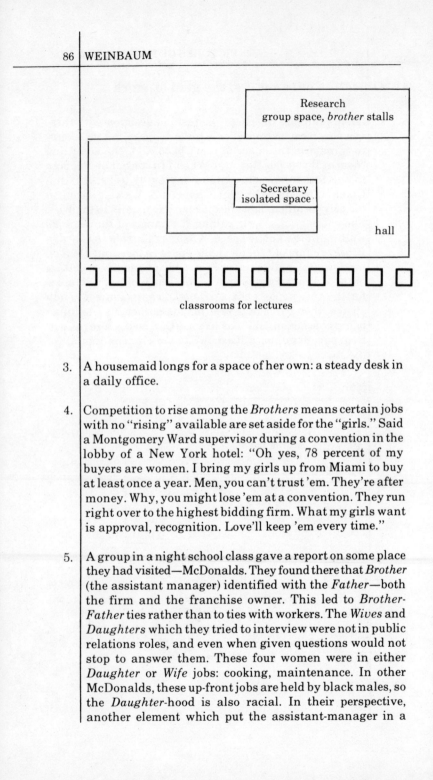

classrooms for lectures

3. A housemaid longs for a space of her own: a steady desk in a daily office.

4. Competition to rise among the *Brothers* means certain jobs with no "rising" available are set aside for the "girls." Said a Montgomery Ward supervisor during a convention in the lobby of a New York hotel: "Oh yes, 78 percent of my buyers are women. I bring my girls up from Miami to buy at least once a year. Men, you can't trust 'em. They're after money. Why, you might lose 'em at a convention. They run right over to the highest bidding firm. What my girls want is approval, recognition. Love'll keep 'em every time."

5. A group in a night school class gave a report on some place they had visited—McDonalds. They found there that *Brother* (the assistant manager) identified with the *Father*—both the firm and the franchise owner. This led to *Brother-Father* ties rather than to ties with workers. The *Wives* and *Daughters* which they tried to interview were not in public relations roles, and even when given questions would not stop to answer them. These four women were in either *Daughter* or *Wife* jobs: cooking, maintenance. In other McDonalds, these up-front jobs are held by black males, so the *Daughter*-hood is also racial. In their perspective, another element which put the assistant-manager in a

broader, more *Father*-identified role was that he was often receiving emergency calls to go attend business in other places, emphasizing Father's cross-workplace interconnecting linkage.

6. From Kurt Vonnegut's *Cat's Cradle*: "Felix ate alone here every day. It was a rule that no one was to sit with him, to interrupt his chain of thought." Felix is a head researcher in a science lab, here a *Father* who has so much space he is never to be interrupted, no matter where he wanders in the plant; as opposed to the secretary whose job it is to *be* interrupted, by clanging of orders, commands, and the phones. This *Father* is a Nobel Laureate in physics at an industrial research lab.

7. Relations between two groups of *Fathers*, illustrated in the persistence of *Daughter*-like characteristics in a *Father*-like job: in one episode of "The Honeymooners," Jackie Gleason, the busdriver, stands around complaining about how some guys just jump when the boss (a regular human being) says he wants something done for him. Gleason maintains he's different. Then Mr. Marshall, the boss, comes back to ask Ralph (Gleason) to teach him to play pool that night. Ralph accepts his offer, but Norton (Art Carney), Ralph's friend, shows up for his pre-arranged game that night. Mr. Marshall assures Ralph that he needn't break his plans, he could do so some other evening, and then invites both Ralph and his friend Norton to come along. While Mr. Marshall leaves to get his car, Carney explains how it's good to socialize with the right people, and explains how he got his current job (in the sewer) on account of the game of golf. (After all, it is among men that the invitation of pool is extended). The man he was caddying for was the butcher. The butcher hit the ball off the golf course and down the sewer, and Norton ran into the foreman. The foreman took a liking to Norton, and offered him a job. "So"—here comes the *Father's* conclusion—"it pays to socialize with the right people." But notice one thing—the rotation of jobs (caddying to sewer) versus the career planning of a more completely characteristic *Father's* job.

8. Sign of interlocking skills of *Fathers*: Ralph, the busdriver on "The Honeymooners" says, "You know that sign they

have in the post office about how the mail gets through, be it rain or snow? That's because the mailman rides with me!"

9. There is a difference between the person and the job: the *Father*-job has security. It is on-going, it will always be there. If he leaves, somebody else will fill it. Whereas with temp help or migrant labor, the insecurity is not individual but structural. A person is hired to fill a temporary function. When grape pickers leave at the end of the summer, nobody is hired as a replacement. There is simply no work there. Thus in an aggregate way there is a great difference.

10. Is a freelancer a *Brother/Father* even though he moves from job to job? Yes, because unlike the roving *Daughter*, the freelancer's job depends on the interlocking skills between groups of *Fathers*—editor of the *Times*, writer for *Newsweek*, etc. Furthermore, the *Brother/Father*-like nature is clearly revealed on the basis of payment. When a freelance photographer is sent to Washington to cover the inauguration, he is given a travel expense perk. Finally the freelance writer or photographer experiences the opposite of the *Daughters'* characteristic invisibility; getting your name around is how you get more assignments both in writing and photography.

11. Sometimes the turning point between a *Brother* and a *Father* job is blurry. Sometimes the turning point is marked more clearly. For example, after a certain point a *Brother* who rises in a bank cannot lose his job once he passes a certain grade level.

12. A woman in a class describes what she identifies as a *Brother* job: counseling in a Catholic maternity home. There were counselors—eight in all—who held master's degrees. The caseworkers held no equivalent degree. They had to work as a team to be sure that none of the clients pitted one worker against another—the cohering nature of work. However, there was also competition among them as to who would stay and who would get promoted. The distinguishing *Brother* characteristic was that each was able to use the experience to negotiate a move elsewhere.

13. At a stuffed animal factory, the head designer in the first room "designed"—developing and directing the conception of his product. He sat at the front of three cutting tables. On either side of the three tables sat one man and one boy— showing how the younger are trained in working relations with older men. One of these men held the material down after they both had rolled the material off the bolts to cut one big size. The older man ploughed across the material with heavy scissors. At the end of the tables, *Wives*, doing "clean-up" tasks, took the big sheets of material and laid the precut patterns on the training paper. In the next room, each woman sat individually sewing up the patterns on her own machine—there was no cooperation of efforts in that each operated her own equipment, no cohering of relations by the nature of trying to get the task done. Next the cut pieces were taken to a third room, where non-English speaking Third World men sat grouped together on a raised platform, cross-legged in the over-crowded space. These men in *Daughter*-jobs exercised a task gener-ated by the *Father* (the designer) two rooms back. They simply turned the sewn animal patterns right side out for stuffing as the pieces were dumped in front of them when the women on the sewing machine were done. In the fourth room, the room in the back, men working machines blew asbestos into the animal pieces, using something like a blow cleaner which shot the hot stuffing into the animal's rear end. The sexual metaphor of that: the men who blew asbestos and hot air into the animal's holes also decorated this same machinery with photographs of women receiv-ing rear phallic penetration. A man then put the blown-up animals into a dryer, as the men in the stuffing room finished them. He rolled them over to a row of women who sewed on the final touches—sewing on round dots for eyes, cheeks, etc. Visually each woman looked like she was dressing a small child. One woman, to illustrate how a woman's job carries the housewife's tasks, brushed down the gorilla's hair. One job—that of a man—had a little more outlet for creativity. He painted on the whiskers of a tiger (the kind you win at Coney Island). He apparently took pleasure in what he was doing, and had turned his back to the rest of the workers to create the illusion of private space. The transistor radio he brought with him also reinforced contours of this illusion.

14.

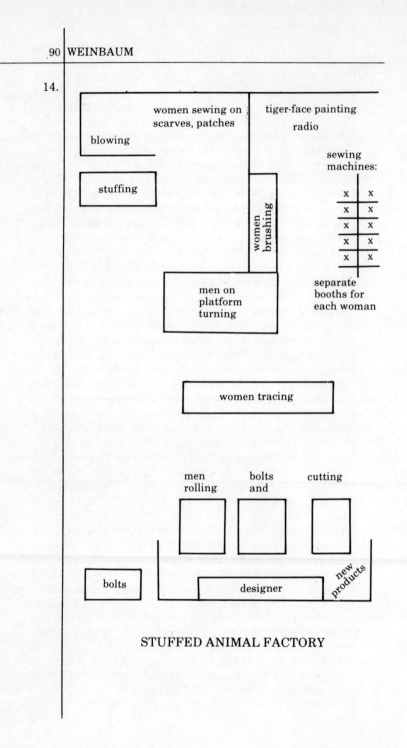

STUFFED ANIMAL FACTORY

15. More on Brooklyn screen and dye, beyond the textual information: In the Brooklyn screen and dye factory, the division of labor was very clear even just within the screening room, Women walked around the long tables, putting up the hangers and placers on tables—a domestic "laying the basis" task. One woman walked along the row and threw the material out; another woman walked around and settled in the screen afterwards. The next step was done by a man: the actual pressing through of the screen which caused the imprint on the material. Predictably, another woman followed this man, cleaning up after the primary task completion. However it must be said that all these are *Daughter* jobs, in relation to the larger structure of corporate production of heavy industry. And also, each of the jobs was *Daughter*-like in terms of no space. Everyone kept walking in circles.

16. Men tending machinery have more freedom to walk up and down the lines, whereas women are like an appendage to the machinery, stuck to it. These women, who couldn't move, would watch the men get together to examine the near completion of the product. The designer—*Father* in the immediate workplace vicinity of a textile factory—gets paid $20 an hour and has to interlock with the managerial level whereas those in *Daughter* jobs never will. The *Father* here has to interlock with other *Fathers* simply by nature of the task—he has to accept feedback to design a saleable sample. This kind of working exchange does not develop with the *Daughters* who sit on one end of the machine putting in the white material over and over, yet again another time. Additionally, the *Father*-designer has material incentives because he has to design a product which sells. *Daughter* has no more material incentive to put in the cloth quicker and quicker. The *Father*-designer (here) was also training a *Brother*. The designer himself identified with the owner, the bigger *Father*.

17. Coders at the Harris opinion polls are *Daughters* in their jobs. First, in terms of reward and relationship to work, they are hired by the hour on the pace of the *Father's* work. As to task assignment, they do that which has been generated elsewhere, calling up people with questions prepared and designed above. One coder I talked to revealed how the psychology of a *Daughter* also operates in the job. Those who worked nights, this coder said, snuck

into the director's office and even took baths in his private bathtub, leaving the cleaning lady (the *Wife*) to clean up after them.

18. Mandatory sexuality on *Daughter*'s job. An ex-foreman in the garment district explained the division of labor. When girls came on the shop they did the cutting and cleaning and folding. The men put the cloth in the machines. The girls got paid a flat rate while the men got wages and material incentives—and additional payment per output. "Now if I had a smart girl in the shop," Reubin the foreman said, "I'd move her up front so she could learn by watching the man work at the machine." Then, after hours, he himself would offer to teach her. Of course this would be on a Friday night, when he'd offer to buy her a meal at the cafeteria. Girl after girl would order nothing more than a cake or coffee, each saying to him, "you work hard for your money, you keep it." That would be the disappointing end of the date. Obviously the date got nothing but sex role training.

19. More mandatory sexuality, more explicitly: in more "advanced" societies, the notion that sexuality is part of survival might seem outrageous. In earlier tribal societies, the connection was more direct. For example according to *Arabesque* Magazine, Aug. 1977, the Ouled Nail is a tribe of Arabs in North Africa who are famous for their belly dancing skills. Their tradition is to hand down the art from mother to daughter. The children are trained at an early age to be professional dancers, and are encouraged to go out as soon as possible to the nearest town to earn a large enough dowry to make a good marriage. Or, in a more "civilized" form of the same institution, *Arabesque*, June 1977, describes: As far back as 1971, when I spent 6 months in the Middle East, performers in the "Waterfront" were being paid 25 to 30 pounds a night. That is the equivalent to $25 to $30 American money in their country. Since that time, with inflation, etc., it has doubled, and let's face it—they triple their salary by working on a commissioned basis. For the uninitiated, this means that the artists sit with customers between performances and usually order champagne—that being the highest costing drink. The performers receive a commission for all that is purchased. Realistically, we know that all performers are not alcoho-

lics, and of course there is a method to this system. Often they are just buying a bottle of bubbly water. This type of employment tradition is common throughout the European continent in places of public entertainment, and it matters not what your professional status is dancewise, meaning that you can be a Spanish dancer, an adajio act, a stripper, etc., and the same rules apply. What our readers also may not realize is that this type of employment does not necessarily mean that you are a practicing prostitute. There are exceptions to all rules, but in most cases, the owners of these establishments maintain a closed-eye policy. In other words, if a person makes special arrangements after the job, this is considered their private business.

20. *D/W* non-cumulative skills versus *Brother's* upward mobility: The immigrant father of a retired elderly woman in one of New York's Jewish cafeterias was in "the garment business." Her brother got a job in a steel plant and worked himself up to head chemist. She got a job in a ladies garment firm as a secretary. Instead of moving up, she married one of the merchandisers in from New York. As she reports, "First time he saw me he said to himself,'I've got to get that girl,' and he came all the way back from New York." He took her on vacation and they eloped. "To look at me now you wouldn't know it," she says, "but I must have been good if after all this time I still hear from my boss." A painful story, one that illustrates how women's sense of their own self-worth is less because men know they are good from their work.

21. As to the fantasy of the *Daughter* escaping workplace humiliation to achieve domestic power in the home: in locker rooms men talking about their wives use the expression "I had a honey do weekend": "Honey do this, honey do that." Women who don't get power at work get it at home. When I gave a lecture at a university once, presenting the grid without the categories until the end, a housewife told me she had identified with all the *Father* characteristics, saying what *he* got at work, *she* got at home.

22. Even a woman trained in a *Brother* field remains a *Wife* on the job. In a study of women lawyers, Cynthia Epstein, sociologist, writes,"Some judges and male colleagues make it particularly unpleasant for women lawyers by question-

ing their competence or ridiculing their attire. Thus some women grow to dislike the courtroom and shun it. Many reported that they were performing the practice's non-legal administrative tasks—hiring secretaries, running the firm's office and keeping the work calendar. These "house-keeping" responsibilities unfortunately do not develop the lawyer's skill or contacts, and may banish her to obscurity.

23. In Ken Kesey's *One Flew Over The Cuckoo's Nest*, Nurse Ratched makes male patients feel "we are the victims of a matriarchy here." She is actually the workplace *Wife*, enforcing rules of the patriarchy in the larger sense. She is enacting rules made by the *Father*, the Psychiatrist, the Doctor.

24. Observations on the unemployment line: If there is an irregularity, *Daughter* sends you to Section C where you have to talk to a *Wife* who has the authority to enforce the *Father's* rules. The lines appear to be doles, but actually the *Brothers* are put into job categories out of which their work must be assigned, so as not to waste training. The segmentation is maintained in the *Daughter/Brother* jobs. The lines themselves are really created for the male job paradigms. The criteria are seldom met by the contours of a *Daughter's* job.

25. In a paper given by Lourdes Beneria at the 1977 American Economics Association, attention was paid to the division between the modern wage versus the petty commodity production sectors. Males were employed in the former, females in the latter, in the areas she studied in the Third World. Women tend to work closer to home, not enjoying much mobility, carrying out tasks which can be integrated with the rearing of children. This leads to lower wages paid to men employed in the capitalist wage sector, a system which can only benefit the "bigger *Fathers*." In Africa, for example, where precapitalist forms of production co-exist with the capitalists, organization of the mines, men work in mining for wages and women are relegated to subsistence farming. This lowers the necessary wage rate paid to men.

26. The same phenomenon appears in *Wife*-like pockets in the middle of fully-developed capitalism too. For example, I once saw cards posted in the laundromat in Brooklyn of a

woman who wanted to teach English to private students on the side. This lowered the necessary rate to her wage-laboring husband too.

27. I have coined the term "metawife work," which means any self-generated employment in the heart of a basically wage-laboring system. A man who sells shirts at the corner, or attendants who work in a parking lot, making the rounds and returning to fill the orders—this might be seen as metawife work too.

28. Planetary patriarchy disciplining the others to follow the *Father's* rules: In Mary Daly's book, *Gyn/Ecology* she coined a few words. One of these was planetary patriarchy. In discussing this concept she gave apt examples of how the *Wife* disciplines others (particularly the *Daughters)* to follow *Father's* rules: the pimps who use older tougher prostitutes to beat up novices. She writes: while these trapped women mete out physical punishment, pimps (like all top-dog bureaucrats) play the role of comforting *Fathers* lovers. Other meta-workplace occurrences of the same phenomenon: the Chinese older women who bound their daughters' feet; the mother-in-law in India who insists the daughter go to suttee (burns herself to death) when the husband dies; the African women who perform cliterectomies on their daughters who otherwise won't attract mates.

29. Whether we are all *Wives* in the larger workplace structures: I saw a cartoon in the *N.Y. Post* once where upon loading rocketship a man in a space suit says to a women in a space suit: "Well, Ms. Higgins, let's run through your duties as a woman astronaut—Wainright here is coffee no cream, Nicholls there is tea with, and I'm plain milk." Historically the subdivision of men's jobs has served as a point of entry for women to the male domains of work. I once saw this mechanism in action while interviewing a unit manager at Metropolitan Life. When asked, "Why hire women in sales?" his response showed how opportunities for women's work are cyclical depending on the state of business in men's affairs. "Everybody knows that in this country, women control home finances," the unit manager smiled. He thought it was "easier for women to talk to wives."

30. Bob, the Metropolitan Life insurance guide, served a large corporation. In talking to me and a group of women, Bob made an effort to develop good public relations. The possibility of recruiting some of us for a sales career with Met Life clearly lurked in his mind and thus seeped through and affected his manner. He was eager to pass out gold-covered job description folders, a stack of which he said he had gathered while preparing for us the previous evening. A unit manager on his way up, Bob was certainly successful in cutting a personable yet sophisticated impression. Without knowing beforehand the inner workings of the entire insurance business, we didn't suspect that the line he was giving us would lead newly-hired women to a raw deal. Channeling women to handle the accounts of private homes frees male representatives to concentrate on more efficient sales to the group plan insurance market. One got the feeling that somewhere a decision had been made—bring in women, yes, (and Bob's unit alone had just hired two), but type-cast them as *Wives*, small parts people, leaving the bigger bits to the men. Any sales rep knows that to earn more he must be efficient. Consequently he reduces the time he must invest in each individual sale to far below that necessitated by home visits. Women, brought in to handle the "home work" geared for the domestic market, free men to approach the heads of business, football teams, and unions to sell them on employees fringe benefit plans.

22. Reinforcement institutions

31. "You're born into the family, where you are given a family role: then you go into the workplace which is structured so that you continue the family role. And in case you didn't get enough of it in the early family, they give you shots of it in advertising, religion, and the media." Two cases in point.

32. When my grandfather died, I rushed into his shul to seek the advice of his rabbi. I asked him what prayers I could say. His answer, a classic: don't worry your head with prayers. Do what your grandfather always wanted. Get married and have children. Or, when in Indiana visiting a

high school mate who had become a "born again Christian"
she told me that if it weren't for being born-again, she
didn't know what would have happened to their marriage.
The religious doctrine set her priorities straight: first God,
then her husband, then children, then everyone else (eg,
friends). What about herself? She submerged herself in the
effort of keeping those handed-down priorities straight.
These reinforcements I am talking about could be diagrammed in the following way:

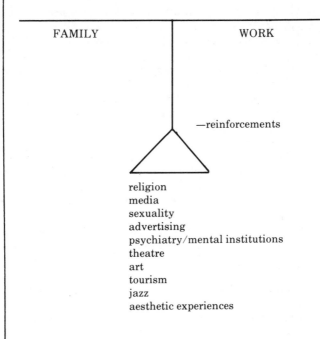

Many of these visual reinforcements have the property for
the viewer of standing on the outside staring into the inner,
into the womb. The way, for example, we stare at products
of creativity with open-mouthed wonderment, suspending
disbelief to be taken in. And what is "on stage" in theatre,
in sports, or in the opera, etc., but the re-enactment of the
primal sex roles. I list tourism because of the quality of the
re-enactment of childhood, being taken in to stare at
society without verbal understanding, as when those in
developed countries opt to visit a "backwards" (and more
sex-role conservative) country. Often on tours, the par-

ticipants are "taken in" to the backrooms of handicraft shops and factories.

33. I list sexuality as a "reinforcement" institution on the notion that if *Fathers* weren't the primary earners (busy, out of the house) *Daughters* wouldn't be heterosexual. Thus let us say that a woman who is trying to throw the socially-designated family role off will, when she turns to satisfy sexual needs with men experience the same pressures of reinforcement.

34. Psychologically, in terms of dynamics behind women's difficulties in jobs and how options available in states of stress merely reinforce them: A woman in her mid 30s was diagnosed as suffering from severe depression, so serious that she was institutionalized and treated with electro-shock therapy. When she came back from the depression, she was almost totally rehabilitated—except for one area. Regarding how she had made a living she had a complete loss of memory.

35. Role of the state: Women get punished if they try to break out of sex roles, and *other* patriarchal institutions (religion, the organization of car technology and the military, the media) intervening if a woman goes too far. Not getting tenure (not getting rewarded) is the same as punishment if you get too far. The image is promoted that a woman is not to succeed in work, but is to get married and have children. A woman succeeding in work is still failing in the sex role. There is no success at all until marrying, in the eyes of the dominant culture. On the other hand, men get special favors for trying to succeed in work such as extra points for veterans (those with families) on the civil service test for mail delivery. No such favors are given to women from their previous or tandem experience in patriarchal insti-tutions. Can you imagine an extra five points given on the post office exam to a woman who has had to undergo mastectomy (male fetishism with The Breast acted out through surgery); a divorce; or who has served a certain number of years as a housewife; mothered a certain number of children leaving a spotty work record; been raped; had her mind fogged with psychoanalytic medica-tion because psychiatrist, family or husband thought her hysterical, depressed or nervous? Certainly not.

23. Other factors: race, class, etc.

36. In Italy, it is common for the "real" fathers to move away for employment to the Western European countries; in which case they adapt the *Daughter* characteristic of moving around from place to place. This shows how in instances of racism, Third World relations and economic crisis the patriarchal privileges get undermined.

37. Other valuable lessons learned while teaching the New Jersey night class: I found myself drawing a grid to show how through a range of classes, the paradigm is also useful to compare differences among *Fathers*. I didn't spend much time on this, since most social theory is about this. The higher you are in the class structure, the point is, the more you exhibit your kin category's characteristics. The *Father* of the ruling class has all *Father* aspects, 1-5. The *Father* of the skilled class maybe 4. *Father* of the unskilled maybe 1-3, etc. The grid I used for the countdown looked like this:

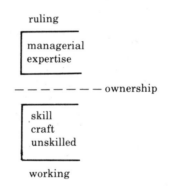

38. What can be seen using such an approach as this is how the truck driver, although by no means the executive, has at least one characteristic setting himself above the clerical worker—his own cab. Class divisions—by which I mean divisions within classes—get reinforced like this.

39. Black male *Daughters*: The post office in N.Y. hires *Daughter* workers during the Christmas season, to conduct people to the stamp windows from the depths of the long lines. These *Daughters* have no space of their own and their work is seasonal. They get no completed work done, whereas at least the seller of the stamps completes his business. The job is much like that of a flyer in a department store or a runner in a hospital running results of tests back and forth from the labs.

40. *Father* to *Daughter* in retirement: *Rhoda*, a television series about a working class family in the Bronx. Her father goes to Fort Lauderdale upon retirement. Explaining why he had "disappeared" from the family in a long-distance call: "what would your mother have said, me running from job to job. I've had eight jobs in three months and my favorite was garbage collecting. I loved waking up rich people."

41. Language/culture: How unfamiliarity with the dominant language puts a biological male into a social *Daughter* position. Ordering a cup of coffee to go in an Italian place in Greenwich Village, I watched a man standing behind the counter being told what to do in Italian by a guy at the end of the counter who was translating my English.

42. Unemployment/economic crisis: the movie, *Sunset Boulevard* illustrates how social categories can be filled by people biologically at odds with their social slots. In the movie, an unemployed male screenwriter named John is hired by the aging movie star Norma Desmond. Norma, who hasn't appeared in a movie since the silent film days, hires him ostensibly to write a script for her to make her debut in the talkies. Norma is aging and decrepit but she lives in luxury. Her home is like a Hollywood screen set: a mansion replete with swimming pools, tile floors, and mahogany winding stairs. In this case, the aging woman is the workplace *Father*. She has a personalized space to work in and feels as much at home as the *Fathers* we saw on the job. She hires the unemployed writer and immediately begins to transform him. She instructs the butler, Max (the workplace *Wife*), to move all of John's belongings out of his apartment and into a room over her garage. She orders Max to stop at an expensive men's store and order a

tuxedo and suits for John. When guests come for a game of bridge, she instructs John to empty her ashtrays (as in the *Father's* work generating the work of others). When John attempts to edit her working manuscript, she throws temper tantrums. None of her scenes must go. Finally, he gives up and becomes her in-house dandy, accepting the contours of the sex role as his job. She gives him no money but she does give him room and board (as a *Daughter* is not paid enough for self-support or support of others). When it rains and the garage roof leaks, Max moves John's belongings into the room next to Norma's (*Daughter* has no space to call her own). There are no locks between their rooms. Finally by New Year's Eve she gives him a gold cigarette case and comes on to him. He refuses to respond to her sexual advances but does as he's bid which is to dance with her.

John tries to leave the house to go to a New Year's Eve Party. Max doesn't want him to upset the mistress. She tries to commit suicide. John returns to her. After all, he has no money, no job, no apartment, no viable connections with other workplace *Daughters*. Where is he to go? She continues to support him. He continues to do as he is told— to dance with her and to flirt with her. Max, the workplace *Wife*, has fake fan letters sent to Norma. He disciplines the *Daughter* constantly. John tries to escape by the traditional escape route of the *Daughter*: marriage. But his fiance marries someone else.

Throughout the movie, Norma is portrayed as neurotic, psychotic, crazy—only because the story portrays the reversal of the standard sex roles. Think, for example, of *Goldfinger*, or *Pygmalion (My Fair Lady)*. The sympathies are for John in this cultural product whereas sex with the servants is common practice as long as the servant is a woman.

43.   Black and white men and black and white women in a nightschool class at a community college quelled within me the ever-nagging question: is this "just a white middle class feminist experience?" One class participant, a young black woman told how she had once worked in a garment factory sewing labels on men's suits. She drew the following workplace diagram:

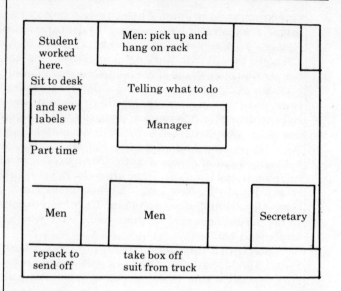

The nature of her work did not allow her to develop any relationship with other workers. Although all the women sat around one table (each with no space to call her own), they did not have to cooperate on a common product together. Each was individually responsible for sewing a label on a suit. Additionally, the coats were imported from Europe. This meant that the entire plant was in a *Wife* "small parts" role in relation to the aggregate structure, as the basic product itself was made elsewhere.

44. Another young black woman worked in a daycare center as a substitute teacher. A summer job, her hours were 7-11 a.m. She was always being shifted around within the workplace. As she was hired only for vacations, she also shifted around between workplaces. She was always working under full-time counselors for minimal wages. The only skill she exercised, as she interpreted it, was that of being the "oldest daughter"—taking care of younger siblings in mother's absence. Still, in the last instance of discipline, Mom herself was called in.

45. A young black male in the class told about his job working for a temp help organization which had recruited him through his high school. The firm, Standby Personnel,

would send him to various workplaces for limited periods of employment at minimum wage. At each place he would take on menial single-task jobs. At Shaston's he cleaned up all night with no one to talk to but the watchman who slept all the time. At Korvette's he played musak over a loud-speaker. At Muir Head, Inc, a paper processing plant, he had to lift heavy rolls of paper to thread through the machinery. Thus the young black male had a job(s) which fit the *Daughter* category: no space of his own, always running around, no chance to rise in the workplace. In the paper processing plant his relation to the product was one of feeding the machinery. The skill required was that of brute strength—not learned on the job but indirectly derived from his sex/"race"/class role.

46. An older white male in the class reported that the phone company hired for manhole jobs in the same way. A trade unionist, he described Ma Bell as "a communications company providing services to the houses and businesses." This gentleman worked in a small outlet servicing the local area. In terms of space, he reported that he took the job because he liked to work outside. You have your own truck, he said, although other people use it occasionally. "It's your workspace when you're there, but others might be given use of the vehicle." He drives the truck around and enters equipment rooms in factories and other places of business. He has a three year contract and can't be fired. A union job, there is automatic progression to top pay if you're there and do the job. He is rewarded through benefits and mileage reimbursement if using his own vehicle. He can also work as much overtime as he wants if he needs more money. He also gets paid holidays and vacations. About skill he reports that "90% of what you learn, you learn on the job—although they do send you to school periodically." The qualifications necessary when you apply are a license, the strength to lift equipment, and sufficient reading and writing ability to work with ma-chinery prints. You have to be able to climb a pole, drive a truck, run wires to fix technical equipment. Knowledge of where to get the parts is helpful, as well as an ability to know how to satisfy the public. Since you have to be available to work overtime if they need you, this job would be harder for women with children.

The workplace *Father's* attitude was clearly demonstrated in this man's talk. "You're pretty well your own boss," he says. "When you're there, nobody bothers you. Once you get in your truck in the morning, the day is yours. No pressure on you. You make your own day." He explained that for the first few months they send you around with "more experienced individuals." Did he use the word "individual" because he was talking to me or was that the normal vocabulary? Have you ever heard "Is there an individual in this typing pool who can get me a cup of coffee?"

He also used the term "grandfathering an individual." This means that nobody is ever actually outdated by new equipment. They get retrained rather than fired. This is a result of having a nearly all-union shop. Only one in 1000 are not.

47. An older black male truckdriver didn't want to testify in the *Father* category on the grounds that he was not an executive. However I encouraged him to talk. As he described his job, the class agreed that several specific factors made his a *Father's* job. His space was his own truck. No one else could drive it. He covered a regular beat or territory and had to get along well with the public or lose the account. Once on his beat, he must call two or three times a day for more pick-ups. Nevertheless the job gave him a relative amount of autonomy and freedom as well as the exploratory opportunity to "meet different kinds of people," which he was proud of. As to relation to work—of course he might go to work one morning only to discover that not enough work is available to be assigned but, as he explained, "If you're up on the seniority list, don't worry." He earns $9 an hour plus overtime and access to a drug benefit through the union. After 15 years he gets longevity—extra pay bonuses. He's also guaranteed holidays as long as he shows up. Concerning skills, he told us you have to be able to haul freight of up to 2000 pounds. If you can't handle it you can call a helper. Being a helper, by the way, is how you get into the job. Young men come in to do shaping, as a helper on a platform. In this way they try to become drivers. Often real fathers get real sons where they work. The only formal entry requirement is having a license allowing you to pull anything behind a regular vehicle such as a tractor. Dock workers get in the same way, he said.

The black driver exhibited *Father* attitudes too. For example, he had the feeling of being indispensable and important. He had the illusion that the owner of the trucking firm "couldn't do the job" without him, as if the owner (or the Big *Father*) depended on his (the driver's) ability to sustain business contacts. I report this as an illusion because the contacts maintained through his beat were actually set up and maintained through a packer's firm. One aspect of the job, however, indicated *Daughterhood*: lifting, a remnant of the skills of heterosexuality maintained on the job. In this case the males' brute strength was a non-job skill supposedly acquired "naturally" by the male.

24. Aggregate implications

48. There are many ways these familial structures reappear even beyond the everyday dynamics of the working situation. Testimony from a union member in a class helped explain how certain terms, such as *grandfathering,* made sense. This particular term applies to people who can't be fired from jobs if a new ruling is passed which eliminates a job category in the future. These men stay in the present because of the past: the patriarchy's privilege to old men. I've never heard of *grandmothering*.

49. Aggregate implications of the kin category perception makes more sense of Third World development and work history. For example, Ivy Pinchbeck in *Women Workers of the Industrial Revolution* tells us:

> Manufacturers were inclined to base wages (to women spinners) on the assumption that the spinners were already maintained by their husband, and at the same time in rural areas, farmers defended the low wages of their laborers on the grounds that women and children supported themselves by spinning. This interdependence of agricultural and spinning wages was a constant source of strife between agri-

culturalists and woolen manufacturers, and reached its culmination point at the end of the (18th) century when the decline of hand spinning made a rise in the laborers' wage imperative.

The agriculturalists were in the petty commodity sphere and the manufacturers in the rising organs of capitalist penetration (sexual innuendo intended). This insight from history clarifies a variation on the same dynamic now occurring in the Third World. Consider, for example, what we can discover from Lourdes Beneria's paper, mentioned earlier. She discusses the modern capitalist wage vs. the petty commodity production spheres, describing how they are split between males and females throughout the Third World. In her studies she found that males dominate the former, females the latter. This pattern results, Beneria asserts, from the fact that women tend to work close to home, not having much mobility, needing to perform tasks which can be integrated with childraising. Even in Africa, where women have their own plots of land, they have to work on men's plots, and the opposite does not take place. Women's subordination to men continues. On plantations (for a wage rate) women work as part-time, not as full-time workers. Where pre-capitalist conditions co-exist with capitalist conditions, women work at a subsistence level and men (in the mines, for example) for wage rates. The income to the household from women's subsistence activity lowers the necessary male wage labor rates. Thus the capitalist miners (the employers) extract more profit from the male (*Father*) workers counting on the *Wife's* existence.

50. More applications to aggregate structure are demonstrated by the fact that *Father* jobs in underdeveloped countries have less of their own space e.g., less *Father*-like characteristics. A book on tourism states: "Tourists from the west have inexhaustible fascination for places such as Istanbul, Tangiers, Damascus and Casablanca where they can see factories without walls." My interpretation is that more of the jobs in the underdeveloped countries have a higher proportion of *Daughter*-like characteristics. As if the countries had been turned inside out since colonial invasion. A higher concentration of *Father*-like jobs in the center of the developed world leaves more *Daughter*-like jobs on the periphery.

51. Booths in the diamond district exhibit family dynamics too. Simply go to New York to observe them (mid-40s in Manhattan, between 5th and 6th avenue). As in the Third World work spaces without walls, the *Father* here has less of his own space too, being a "petty commodity/family mode" pocket in an advanced capitalist country.

25. Experience and consciousness of roles: the actor's perceptions

52. On feminization of jobs: Is it the job, the actual position, or the sex of the person who fills it? A friend of mine, a biologist in a university in Italy, had the problem that students didn't want to be in a study group with her because they felt that they were going behind the director's back. They didn't want to come to her, to be disloyal to him. Their mama and papa conflicts emerged, making it difficult for her to get along professionally within the institution, especially vis-a-vis her colleagues.

    Because jobs do have characteristics that can fit into one job role as well as another, the attitude you bring determines the outcome as much as the actual response of others to you. If you bring a biological daughter's attitude to a job which would be interpreted differently by a biological brother, you might reshape the contours of the job. This might then occur on an aggregate level the way the doctor's role, once filled by women in the Soviet union, has turned from *Father* to *Wife*.

53. A good idea for class experiment: take one job and talk it all the way through with different consciousnesses. In one class a female pastor looked at her job as a *Father*, then as a *Wife*. With each sample categorization new insights occurred to her. Each job could go one way or the other depending on your attitude—which in turn got instilled in early childhood.

54. An older woman worked on one register in a cafeteria, a young man from Argentina on another. She took it as a

a grocery chain elsewhere. To him it was one link in the food industry and he pulled himself up on the chain.

55. All roles are relative: for example, a manager in Gino's is *Father* to the local workers at the same time that he is *Wife* to the larger *Father*, enforcing the corporate rules. Or, the local manager can be seen as a *Brother*, being prepared for rising higher in the corporate structure. Of course, there is a contradiction between the psycho-sexual derivation of the categories and the "simple" way in which a man can appear in a *Wife* slot, since when a man is performing a *Wife* or *Daughter* role he is being emasculated by that slot. This has all kinds of implications for how that male worker sees himself and is seen by others.

56. The definition of a role depends on one's perspective. For example, I once had a job in a college women's program. The women's center and the women's studies people applied for a continuing education grant. With this money, separate jobs were created to carry out the goals of the grant. Most of us were hired part-time; only two of the administrative positions were full-time. Those who directed the grant appeared to us as *Fathers*, yet the directors saw themselves as *Daughters* vis-a-vis the rest of the academic world.

57. Leaving a job is like leaving the family; like birth (leaving the womb); like death (leaving life). Given the number of times a *Daughter* is leaving a job, she's undergoing separation anxiety constantly.

58. Love or interconnectedness to others in *Brother/ Father* jobs: the feeling of being linked through professional organization. A simple research job is not so bad because elsewhere (outside the workplace) other people respect you.

59. *The New Yorker* (13 June 1977) tells the story of one of the first "girls" to take on the job of copy "boy." The job of the copy "person" is to carry copy from desk to desk. This "carrying" occurs in the city room, an enormous room consisting of various regions filled with desks. In the center of the room is a long bench—the copy boys' bench. Copy boys sit there and wait for a summons. When a voice shouts "Boy!" from any of the regions, a boy is supposed to

rise, go swiftly to the person who called, take whatever is handed to him, and carry it where it is supposed to go. These "boys" will rise to reporter, or hope to, and therefore will follow any orders of the boss. *Daughters* in such positions find various ways of rebelling. Often they have trouble following the rules—and why should they? They don't hope to rise within the structure but to be married and out.

60. There is a different psychology for *Brother* and *Daughter*; there is also a distinction between *Father* and *Wife*. This distinction emerges both in the workplace and in private life. For example, a woman working in a cafeteria commented that it doesn't matter what you do, as long as you do it for someone you care for. I immediately spotted a *Wife's* perspective. "But," I asked her, "don't you want to find meaningful work?" She replied: "Doing menial work for people you care for *is* meaningful."

61. In *Herzog* by Saul Bellow, the major character, a professor, was going through an intense mid-life crisis. The narrator commented: "To look for fulfillment in another, in interpersonal relations, was a feminine game. And the man who shops from woman to woman, though his heart aches with idealism, with the desire for pure love—has entered the female realm." Later on he comments, "I am going through a change of outlook...I find I've been working for others, for a number of ladies...developing the psychology of a run-away slave." The psychology of the slave equals the psychology of the wife.

62. I am often asked: What is the disjuncture between *Daughter* and *Wife*? Within the objective structure, the *Daughter/ Wife* distinction depends on the attitude of the woman. Has she realized the full consequences of her difference from men? Does she realize yet what the future holds, and does she have to act out her fantasy to prepare for it?

63. Contrasting the workplace attitude of *Daughter* and *Wife*: Three women worked in a dentist's office: a dental assistant, a dental hygienist, and a secretary/receptionist. The latter, the workplace *Wife*, played the role of disciplining other workers. For instance, she once told the dental

assistant to get off the phone. The workplace *Wife* worked there full-time. The other two were part-timers. The dental hygienist was proud of the fact that she could go from office to office, taking her *Brother*-like skills two days a week here, two days a week there. The hygienist took the exercise of her skills seriously, but observed how negligent the assistant was about her job: "What does she care, its Daddy's money."

64. The *Wife*-like attitude of doing something menial for people you care for often transports to exploiting those who hold that attitude: it's for the movement, it's for God and the church, it's for women in general, or women in a program at a college, it's for the cause. This directly contrast to the menial alienation attitude which creeps into the *Daughter* at work. For example, the woman who described her first job at a department store was responsible for calling people who were behind on their bills. She treated it as a lark, putting on a different accent with each call: French, southern, Italian, German.

65. A *Brother's* approach to work: A tycoon in a widely-watched television soap opera started off in an orphanage. He was a dishwasher one summer in a hotel and made a nuisance of himself watching and asking questions of a cook. He was made a cook's assistant and they hired a new dishwasher. He was always looking at every job as a training job—what could he learn from it.

66. One block down from where I used to live there was a family-owned stationery store. I interviewed the book-keeper after old man Murray, the original owner, died. Murray had left Harold, his business partner, the entire business. The bookkeeper complained that Harold was having trouble locating another partner. He had hired a young boy to do the shipping, one of Murray's many tasks, thus creating a *Daughter* job to relieve some of the temporary *Father* (partner) burden. The bookkeeper—a woman—was obviously a person well-versed in the ins-and-outs of the business, yet she remained a bookkeeper. I asked, "So why don't you become his partner?" She said, "I'm his sister." "So?" "Well nine-tenths of the time Harold's gone. He needs someone to stay here, to oversee everything while he's not at home." "Why don't you

become his partner," I pushed again. "I'm his sister! I'm well taken care of. My job is secure. End of the year I get a bonus. As long as I'm well he can't fire me." She prefers this set-up to when she was younger working in an office. "You are just another number after a while" she reminisces.

To give an idea about the current arrangement of jobs, she does the bookkeeping; three times a week a "boy" comes in to post bills (stick them in her book) and do the filing and shipping. Harold runs around interconnecting with a lot of *Fathers* in New Jersey, Long Island and the suburban shops. Only 10 percent of the business is over the counter.

The line of descending ownership at various stages of the shop history is interesting in terms of family roles too. Murray (the just deceased) came into the store through his sister. It was her husband's place. When he died, Murray came in "to take care of his sister." Then Harold eventually bought her out. She came in only when she wanted to work.

When I asked why the paste-up boy wasn't trained to be the partner I was told "This is a small place—there's no moving up. Besides, he's part-time. He's studying at N.Y.U."

When I mentioned that I worked at Brooklyn College she commented: "We used to get our help from there." Thus the shop perpetually generates *Daughter* jobs.

67. Domestic duties are often piled automatically and unreasonably onto the *Wife's* job: For example, take the pretzel booth under Grand Central Station. The woman is in the front selling; the man is in the back putting dough into the machine. She's angry that *Father* also expects her to scrub the place. "People wanna buy pretzels from a girl whose dirty? No! Man's nuts!" she said.

68. Psychology of the *Daughter*. You know how when you visit your mother's house, if you put things down in one place she'll automatically move them to another? This is also an irritation the workplace *Daughter* knows well: the constant control of work space exercised by supervisors and administrators who determine what clothes we can wear, what chair we can sit in, what food we can eat, where we can hang our coats, where we can smoke, where all the essential implements of a job—pen, paper, paperclips, rubber bands—will be stored.

69. Building on Nancy Chodorow's thesis about who the father represents in the nuclear family, further thoughts occurred to me. Mother represents powerlessness, the father represents power as he has power when he comes in from the outside. The mother tries to make the child grow up. The father comes in and treats the child like a baby. This is especially true of how the father treats the daughter. The mother is the discipliner while the father is playful. When *Daughter* goes out, then, she becomes playful. Therefore she doesn't "act serious" at work. She maintains a certain playfulness about money, the business of earning a living!

70. In some ways *Daughter's* marginalization can give her more political room to move. Her less secure and less prestigious position means she has less to lose. Two examples: A medical laboratory was being unionized. Most of this organizing was done by a receptionist *(Daughter)*. The more skilled people tended to work longer years, whereas her job had high turnover. The long-term workers felt more firm loyalty than she did. And secondly, the post office in N.Y.C. hires *Daughters* during Christmas rush. This group of workers played a major role during a strike, whereas full-timers were restricted by union rules prohibiting strike activity for the first 6 years of employment.

26. Sexuality of work and money; psychic symbolism imparted to us via the family

71. According to Freud, "Happiness comes from the fulfillment of pre-historic needs. Therefore wealth brings no happiness. Money is not an infantile wish." In the system of unconscious imagery proposed by Freud, money symbolizes excrement to the animal underneath the human psyche. This father of free association explained his sense of unconscious in the equation money = shit. The best developed examples are found in his analysis of Dostoevsky and Leonardo Da Vinci. The latter was a man so anal in his relation to [money = shit] that he saved all his receipts

and bills for supplies, making detailed entries of every monetary transaction in his journals. While most modern/ neo-Freudians agree to feeling that something about money must be "dirty" they have done little with it. Norman C. Brown, for example, places the money = shit equation into a more popular expression "filthy lucre." Certainly not adequate for the purposes of radical feminism.

72. More on sex and money: the main character in Francine du Plessix Gray's *Lovers and Tyrants* describes how her girl friend lives in a house where her parents discuss "makes of watches, bridge-bidding situations, burglar alarms, the truth about meat tenderizers, and other people's money." The main character goes on: "When we were 12, in the seventh grade, we got the curse. 'I used up the whole box of kotex over the weekend,' she [the girl friend] said superciliously. I despaired in silence. It was one more asset she had over me. She always had pretty clothes, popularity, and all those chevrons, pots of money, the best pack of tarot cards in town and now she had the curse."

As I said, admitting to the feeling that there might be something dirty about money, something that might even have been ordered and structured and discussed and disseminated throughout civilization since the time of Leonardo Da Vinci, I noticed in my readings of Freud that most of the symbolism was developed from the unconscious of men. To the female unconscious, that is, the unconscious of the *Daughter*—for it is as a daughter that all women begin—money is dirty. Perhaps even dirtier than it is to men.

73. More on the theme: In reading more Freud, I came across an equation that equated a baby with a penis. A man gives his woman his penis; the woman presents the baby to the man. Having collected so many of the theoretical observations that somehow linked sex and sexuality with money, I began to turn over the symbolism in the form of money-giving rituals. Money, dirty, sexuality—of course. Could money stand for or unconsciously represent the (dirty) ejaculation given to woman by man? Could money represent semen? As in the best bred, the most money. The most money purchases the best semen.

74. On the illicit connection between sex and $: Erica Jong

describes how she felt after sleeping with her lover in *How to Save Your Own Life,*

> Usually I felt wonderful after an assignation. Before I would be tense, obsessive, terrified. I'd call Bennet [her husband] at the hospital and be exceedingly sweet to him and also set up my alibi for the afternoon. "I'm going to Blooming-dale's, darling," I'd say, quite unconsciously confirming the deep connection between sex and shopping, between Bloom and Bloomingdale's... all those women promiscuously spending money, stuffing bags with things, charging, charging to their husband's accounts, were starved for sex! So many holes to fill. So much misplaced passion!

75. Jong uses the image of a big penis spouting money elsewhere when she describes her fantasy of the zipless fuck in *Fear of Flying.* Considering the ritualized form of money-giving most apparent to children in the early years, I am not surprised that a certain eroticism gets absorbed. In the core oedipal structure, after all, mother stays home and does primary parenting and father goes out of the home to being money back in. He presents the money as he presents his sex (from the child's point of view) to the mother. Thus an unconscious equation could be easily created: [$ = S] or money is similar or equal to sex. This could also be expressed [S & M] or there is a deep connection between sex and money.

76. Although the above equations were created by looking at what father gives to mother from the point of view of the daughter, the connection occurs in the minds of men too. In Gail Godwin's *The Odd Woman*, the main character asks her stepfather for money to get to New York. He gives her $500, more than she needs or asks for, and tells her not to let her mother know. He assumes it is for an abortion.

In Tilmann Moser's *Fragments of an Analysis*, he discusses the pleasurable feeling of mixing his sperm with the sperm of other men when he visits a prostitute; the pleasurable feeling is derived by the mixing of money also, when paying her.

Saul Bellow writes in *Herzog*: "A woman who squanders her husband's money, all agreed, was determined to castrate him."

77. Novelists and poets rarely define or label symbols; they merely create them in the struggle to depict the essence of life accurately. Which gives us access to un-categorized levels of the unconscious, so it's quite all right. Doris Lessing writes in *The Golden Notebook*:

> He said, as he dressed: "I can't see you tonight, Ella." She said without fear: "Well, that's all right." But he went on, laughing," After all, I've got to see my children sometime." It sounded as if he were accusing her of deliberately keeping him from them. "But I haven't stopped you," said Ella. "Oh yes you have," he said, half singing it. He kissed her lightly, laughing, on the forehead. That's how he kissed his other women, she thought, when he left them for good. Yes, he didn't care about them, and he laughed and kissed them on the forehead. And suddenly a picture came into mind, at which she started, astonished. She saw him putting his money onto a mantle piece. Yes, it was something implicit in the sort of man who would pay for a woman. Yes, yet, she could see him, clearly, putting money on a mantle piece. Yes, It was something implicit in his attitude.

The female teenage character portrayed by Joyce Carol Oates in *Them*: As she is being driven to a motel to sleep with a man, she looks out a window and sees images of money coming and going, shopping and spending— almost as waves of the ocean hitting the shore and rolling out and back in again, *she sees money as a fluid substance going from hand to hand.*

Marge Piercy writes in her poem "You Ask Why":

> If you turn over the old
> refuse of *sexual slurs*,
> The worn button of
> language, you find
> men talking of *spending* and
> women of *dying*.*

*From *The 12 Spoken Wheel Flashing.*

78. Sexual connotations of money from the point of view of men: David Susskind interviewing Mel Brooks, George Segal and other successful Jewish sons in show business. Brooks says to Susskind, "How much do you give her (his mother), David? A month? Is she happy with it?" Susskind responds: "She's thrilled."

Mel Brooks goes on: "Jewish girls want to see you leave a big tip—a meal costs $32.50 and they want to see you leave $7.00, as a gesture, and then they say, no, $2.00 is enough..."

And one last quip: "In the Jewish religion you have to pay alimony after going with a girl and shaking hands. Not much, just a token, 80 percent, but you have to give something."

79. Sexual symbolism in alimony disputes. An exchange between a man and his lawyer:

> "All right I'll settle for this much a month."
> "OK."
> "I'm getting screwed."

80. Sex and money are tied from the get-go:

> "Do you So-and-So, Daughter of So-and-So, promise not to conceal earnings or income from the groom should he become your 'ex' in the case of divorce?"
> "I do."
> "And do you, So-and-So, Son of So-and-So, hereby swear to contribute 15 percent of your earnings to this bride should she become your 'ex' in case of divorce?"
> "I do."
> "And to contribute 25 percent if the divorce is due to infidelity on your part?"
> "..."
> "I asked you a question, groom."
> "(Gulp) I do."
> "And do you, So-and-So, promise not to sue for the exotic dog?"

81. Money as sexual vulnerability for those who don't admit it: A man picking up a hitch hiker hides his money, figuring he has ten dollars to lose. A woman picking up a man in a bar takes him home. The statement is made, "Why, you are

very brave." Her response: "Well, when I went out to the living room I hid my money."

82. Sex and money in dreams: The second night I slept with J—, I had a dream that my cunt was lined with money inside. I opened my legs and out came a sexy shimmering First National City Bank pillow. D— and J—, the electrician and the assistant, were there to catch it. The bank pillow was red and white satin. The first time I slept without him, I woke up scheming how I could write grants, raise money, finance my next theoretical book—about sex and age roles, family relationships in the economy.

83. A dream: me in a slum apartment, a man with class, status and power coming to make love to/with me. Do I have to stay poor—in need of money—to be attractive to men? Is this eroticism of money really an *oppressed* consciousness? How have I internalized what it takes to be sexually attractive?

84. All (hetero)sexual relations (across race, class and cultural differences) hit the money nexus in some form: A second generation Italian businessman remarked how his partner "screwed" him, complaining that his partner "used to get his rocks off by carrying thousand dollar checks in his pocket." The businessman asked his partner "why don't you get yourself a broad?"

What purpose would the "broad" serve? To get his "rocks off" or to save his money? I didn't ask but remembered a handyman (Puerto Rican) who used to give his bank book to his girl friend so he couldn't go on a spending spree and blow it; or a man (Italian) whose mother used to say that she should get him to take his money and put it in a bank account or buy health insurance. Instead he used to keep it in barrels of different denominations of coins around the house. The common denominator: the woman in a money relationship to the man.

85. Karen Horney in *Feminine Psychology* describes the marked difference in the psychology of men and women. In the average case, Horney says sexuality in women is much more closely tied up with tenderness, with feelings, and affection than in men. An average man will not be

impotent even when he does not feel any particular tenderness for the woman. On the contrary, there is very often a split between sex life and love life so that in extremely pathological situations a man can only have sexual relations with a woman whom he does not care for and can feel no sexual desire for often he is impotent toward a woman he really likes.

Men who have this relation to women substitute giving money for giving sex, which leaves women frustrated, because being the recipient of sex-charged money is always a turn-on. Or, in a reversal, men feel guilty about owing women money when what they owe is sex.

86. A poor struggling actress in New York spends a weekend with an old high school friend. He is now earning $25,000 a year. Every time she thinks of this when making love with him she gets extremely turned-on.

87. Sexual orgasms and money: A small businessman didn't like to be refered to as "small." Although technically an owner of a couple of shops, he took this to be an insulting remark referring to the size of his penis.

88. In Chekhov's play *The Cherry Orchard*, the perpetual student stands on a ladder and throws money down while he talks about how he is "above love." He is "above love" and doesn't want to have anything to do with money.

89. Men giving their sperm and money to women: Once a man told me "all he contributed was the cash" when he got a woman pregnant. Some one else I knew used to brag how he had "dropped plenty of kids around" the way men "drop" money. Sexually "loose" women are more apt than others to leave money lying loose around the house while more rigid ("frigid") women save it; the disciplining, sexually repressed, domesticating women encourage men to save money.

90. On castration: A divorced man used to complain that his ex-father-in-law wouldn't let him pay his share of the dinner bill when they went out. A few years into Freudian analysis, he spoke of his father-in-law as being "castrating."

91. Sublimated sexual ties between men over ties of money. In
     Fragments of An Analysis, Tilman Moser discusses his
     feelings about visiting a prostitute. A psychoanalyst in
     training, the book is an account of his apprenticeship on
     the couch. Moser recalls in vivid emotional detail the deep
     pleasure he felt in the knowledge that his sperm mixed
     with the sperm of money inside the body of the woman.
     That is, woman as vehicle rather than woman as self. Each
     of their deposits of sperm pool inside the woman, as each of
     their deposits of money pool through her. In this context,
     the male pooling, pondering over and planning about
     money takes on a sublimated (homo) sexual hue. Think
     about the constant discussions among men, and see the
     excitement they put into them: the stock market, the race
     track, pension funds, how to get a job, receipts, bills, per-
     centiles for social security taxes. It seems that most men
     would rather discuss money with other men than with
     women in their own families.

92. "Money is like a man's wife—strangers should keep their
     hands off it," says the father character in *Flower Drum
     Song*. His money was stolen from under his bed in San
     Francisco's Chinatown. He is explaining why he refused to
     deposit his money in the bank.

93. Illicit earnings of money by the wife: In *Madame Bovary,*
     her extra-marital and independent financial affairs begin
     at the same time. Does she feel as guilty about selling
     trinkets for money as she does about taking a lover?

94. In "The Honeymooners" television show when Ralph
     Cramden's wife, Alice, gets a job as a babysitter, Ralph
     suspects her of having an affair. Why is Alice's desire to
     earn money automatically linked with sexual infidelity in
     Ralph's mind?

95. More sex-money riffs from "The Honeymooners": In one
     episode, Ralph gets laid off. The interchange that follows
     is laden with sex and $ innuendo. Ralph says to Alice,
     "This is an emergency situation. Let's add together all the
     money we have—Christmas Club, War Bonds, all the
     money you have *hidden* around here." His tone on the last
     phrase is accusatory. Alice protests and shouts, "How
     much do you think I can buy on $62 a week?" "Will you stop
     that?" he implores. "I don't want all the neighbors to

know. I don't want it to *leak* out." Alice sarcastically says, "Ralph, your salary couldn't *drip* out." "Alice," he roars, "you are *flirting* with death." Thus the discussion about money becomes explicitly sexual.

The episode continues. Alice gets a job as a secretary. Ralph cannot find work. Alice comes home for dinner and says she has to return to do inventory that *night*. Ralph's upset. Then he finds out she's the only girl in the office. Ralph gets jealous. Alice has told her boss, Tony, that she lives with her brother. She couldn't very well tell him she's married because it's against office rules. The rule was made to prevent married men from making their wives quit.

Ralph, in a sulk, is visited by the upstairs neighbor, Norton, who asks Ralph if he is depressed about not having a job. "It's not the lay-off, Norton," answers Ralph. "It's that job Alice has gotten. Boss thinks she's single, he'll try to make a date with her."

The boss comes to pick up Alice. He's handsome. Norton tears up the job application he was going to mail for his wife, Trixie. Ralph threatens to tear up Alice's working papers. "What's the matter, Ralph," Alice asks. "Don't you trust me?" "I trust you, Alice," Ralph answers. "I don't trust him." Ralph makes them both stay there in the apartment to work rather than going back to the office that night. As soon as he gets the news that he's got his job back, Ralph throws Alice's boss out. In the end, Alice is moved, telling Ralph how much she loves him. "It's not every woman who, after being married 25 years, has a husband this jealous."

96. Money as a mysterious ephemeral substance: Again on "The Honeymooners" when Ralph thinks he will inherit $40 million, Norton brings a suitcase to the reading of the will. "Why?" Ralph asks. Norton answers, "You can't take $40 million home in your pocket." Here the size of money is talked about in the same way as a man's penis—sometimes big, sometimes small.

97. Male bonding around money: Ralph gives money to Alice for her to keep for him. One day he begs her to let him have it to pay dues to his all-male club. A sublimated transference of primary sexual energy.

98. Workplace sex/money symbolism: I have noticed that there are two major sources of giving money. When a child, you get it from the family. When an adult, from an employer. What feelings does this induce. I have had friends be obedient to me because I have lent them money. I have felt it my responsibility to "live up" to people who have lent me money. The same feelings initiated in the family, transfer to the workplace.

99. Money to women from men is similar to money to *Daughter* from *Father*. This transaction is as threatening to *Daughter* as food from women is to men—food from women symbolizing love from mother.

100. Group rituals cohere individuals into a collective spermadic fluid by pooling of money. This occurs in different classes, religions, daily life incidences and cultures. For example, Saul Bellow writes in *Herzog* of a character who, on his way to meet a lover, drops his subway fare into a slot where he sees a whole series of tokens lighted from within and magnified by the glass. Innumerable millions of passengers had polished the wood of the turnstyle with their hips. From this arose a feeling of communion—brotherhood. This was serious, thought Herzog, as he passed through. The creation of brotherhood by the mixing of money.

101. More group money rituals: money can be a symbolic union imparting the "part of a larger group" feeling: There used to be a woman who would hold court every April in a cafeteria. Other workers from the garment district would come from miles around and have her help fill out their tax forms. She didn't charge for this service because, as she said, "I'm not a woman like that."

102. On morning I came up from the subway and was struck by two money rituals: a nun stood at the top of the stairs and Catholics dropped money in her cup as they shuffled past. Similarly, at the Merrill Lynch booth in the middle of the station, men in business suits and gray felt hats waited to get inside the booth and find out information about their stocks by pushing buttons on a computer terminal. The way they congregated, shuffling in line as others passed, seemed strangely like the way orthodox Jewish men stop at a shul on the way to work to *davin*. Here we have a religious tying to a larger group through money.

103. Comparing two forms of Jewish money raising rituals: the Orthodox Jews, known for being more primitive, uncouth and sexual make more of ritual participation at the New Year. At the end of the services, each family name is called and the women in the balcony catch the eye of the fathers on the pews below, signalling amounts or indicating agreement. It appears to be a sexual back and forth, a flirtation between men and women who are tied sexually around a financial decision. The amount to be given is called out, the biggest amount getting the biggest response from the congregation. In Gramercy Park, on the other hand, in a conservative shul the environment is more repressed. At the end of the New Year services, a request from the pulpit is discretely made and congregants are left to send unannounced checks on their own.

104. Money/sexual symbolism/religion: Many public money-giving rituals happen in the fall. At the San Ginero festival in Little Italy, Mulberry Street is covered with stalls selling sausages, wine, game throws, etc. A shrine of a female saint is pulled on a float down the center of the street. The float is followed by men in black suits and a brass band. The procession comes to a halt before each stall while the band plays. The stall keeper must run forward and contribute money by pinning the bills or checks all over the female saint's body.

105. Symbolism of money: In bars, people who are "loose" with money are likewise considered "loose" sexually.

106. The illicit sexuality of money: Diane Wakoski in *The Motorcycle Betrayal Poems* writes:

> I tail the one I love
> The man who's taken millions
> from the Chemical Trust.
> (Don't
> they say,
> "when a woman's needs are financial,
> her reaction is chemical?"

107. Sexuality at the job interview is portrayed in this scene titled "Gee, You're Not Anything."

"Gee you're not anything like we pictured on the phone."

"Pardon? Now that we're alone face to face in this famous place, could you be a bit more clear—about what you want done here?"

"Well, you know, more hair—"

"Well, I just cut it off for the summer."

"Less of a stare—"

"Well, I'm busy taking it all in, I don't, usually—"

"I thought—perhaps—more—"

"More what? More...pose? Repose? More toes? Yes. I usually have more toes. 12. I usually have 12 toes. 12 more toes. You know how things goes."

And what's that on your nose?"

"Sunburn. Yes. Right now I have sunburn. I do burn a bit on the nose. But just in the summer."

"Ahem yes well. That could be fixed, we know. So, down here—"

"Down where? Oh. Down there. Yes. I usually have more hair. But I was posing for *Playgirl Magazine.* I pose sometimes for money, isn't it funny. Tee hee. But down there, it's true, I usually do have more hair. Much, much more *more* hair. Down there."

"There, there you mean THERE? That's nice to know, I meant, we don't care. Now, I meant, down here—on your resume. Where it lists your, what shall I say, 'experience.'"

"Oh yes. I forgot. What I sent here. What—what does it say? Can you tell me? I sent out so many that day—each slanted a different way."

"Well. It's very impressive. It says 'Experience: 721.'"

"Yes. Oh yes. I've done 721.

"721 *what?*"

"Why 721 job interviews. Oh yes. I've had a lot of *very impressive* job interviews, and it's all been *such fun.*"

"But when we say 'experience,' we usually mean experience at *jobs,* not at *interviews.*"

"I don't care what we usually mean. They are not handing out jobs nowadays. What else can I say. Experience: 721."

"Tell me. How many places have you sent your resume?"

"Well! What are you trying to say! I don't just send it indiscriminately to *strangers!* That would be so indecent, anyway! Letting all those people I don't even know look at my resume! I say! What on earth do you think I am? I wouldn't show my resume to *anyone!* Just because I'm in such a god damn economic *jam!*"

"Well, they have these places, you know, central places, where you send resumes, and then people all over the country, they look at your resume."

"Well, god damn you, you dirty old fool. Just because I show you my resume once, you carry on that way! You demand the right to know who else has seen my resume! What gives *you* the right to know! I'd never ask you that, you know!"

"Well, I just wanted to know—"

"I don't care *what* you wanted to know! Now go! Go out there and later we'll let you know! What we think of *your* resume. Oh, I see. Your resume is a private affair. Well. The rich can afford their privacy. We, on the other hand, wouldn't dare conceal our hair. Or let on that we care that all these strangers—see us—down that—way—so—bare."

108. Once at work, the consciousness of women is not that they have become women, but that they are daddy's little girls. Mike Nichols and Elaine May satirize a boss taking out a secretary:

"Uh, what are you going to be drinking, Miss Lemas?"

"Umm, oh, uh, gee—I don't know—"

"I bet you'd like a brandy Alexander—most ladies really go for them."

"Is that with cream, and, uh? That's a bit rich for me."

"Rich, uh, yah—why don't I just order for you. Morris, bring us a couple of rye and ginger ales. Canadian Club...Listen I wanted to commend you, Miss Lemas. That was a first rate number one job you did on that whole mimeo deal."

"Oh, thank you."

"Yes, it really was. I was going to tell you, but I didn't want to say it in front of the other girls. You know, you start that stuff..."

"Oh, no. Well, I mean you know it was easy you know. I just mimeographed..."

"Thanks, Morris. Yah, go on honey."

"Oh, nothing. It's just that I mean I'll see some of the

girls running a copy off on the mimeograph, and it's just that I'll see it's running out of ink. And sometimes I go up to them..."

"Yah, what the hell."

"...and say, 'it's running out of ink, you should ink it,' and a lot of times they just won't!"

"You know..."

"It's not that they don't *want* to..."

"I don't understand. I just don't understand it. I think that we're a *happy* family and girls like yourself, Miss Lemas, that sort of have *that* feeling we are all together, pulling together..."

"I do really, yah, it's...This drink is very good."

"Cause that's the kind of feeling we like our girls to get. Drink up, honey."

"You know, I—I, I mean, it's so nice you know, for me I mean, working at GAA and P. Because I never thought you know when I got out of school...I mean I never thought I'd just really get into a place where I felt so much at home..."

"I'm glad you do, sweetheart. I mean I really am. We like having you."

"Oh, I just love it there, I really do. I mean I think it's so important—you know—"

"You like Andre Kostelanetz?"

"Um, well, I mostly, I uh, I listen mostly to semi-classical music."

"Yah, I mean—well, that's what this is. I got a new record from the record of the month club. They send me a lot of this semi-class stuff, and, uh, I got a new record. I've got a big hifi. I thought, if you like that kind of stuff. I was gonna see if you'd like to hear—just a snatch of it..."

"I, uh, well, what's it called?"

"Just *Andre Kostelanetz Plays Footlight Favorites,* is what it is. Would you like to come up and hear a little bit of it."

"Uh, into your apartment?"

"Ya, well, that's where the hifi is."

"I didn't think it was in the street."

"You want to honey?"

"Well, uh, wouldn't your wife mind?"

"Uh, no, well she's up in the mountains. See she takes the kids to the mountains. I just rattle around this whole place by myself. This whole big apartment."

"Oh, yah, it's just really, I'm sorry...is that your foot?"

"Ha! Sorry, I thought it was the table. It's, uh."

"That's all right. I didn't mind. I just didn't know if you knew—I thought it was..."

"So, uh, what do you say we could just go up there, give the record a whirl—I think you'd like it."

"Well, uh, I have to be home early."

"Yah, well, we'll get you right home. We'll get you right home."

"I'd have to catch a train."

"Right, right."

"I, I think I would enjoy listening to the music..."

"Swell, O.K. We'll, uh...Morris, uh, check! Thanks, fellah. That'll be it."

"I've heard a lot about him, Andre Kostelanetz."

"Yah, well, I think you'll like it. I really do."

"O.K."

"O.K."

In this skit, the boss plays into the unconscious fantasy of woman as worker. He does so by making references to the office as "one big happy family." He speaks of "our girls" the way a father speaks of children. He compliments Miss Lemas on her work and appeals to symbolic sibling. She responds to the flattery. He mentions that his wife is away and invites her back to the apartment. As last she gets Daddy without Mommy. In some sense, then, these incestuous fantasies of the little girl who wants to sleep with her father (and vice versa) are given a chance to be acted out in the structure of work which duplicates the structure of the family.

109. Another fantasy acting out of compulsive heterosexual behavior from a *Playgirl Magazine* story called "At the Office."

You've had this job for several months. You're an efficient secretary who enjoys her work, although sometimes you wished the men in your office wouldn't ogle your voluptuous figure so openly.

You've even caught your own boss, Mr. Marshall admiring you. You ignored it, but secretly you think he's cute.

One day, while you are sitting at your typewriter, Mr. Marshall walks over to your desk. He says he's come to look for something he left in your bottom drawer the night before.

"Don't bother to move," he says as you start to get up.

So you go back to your typing. He bends down and rifles some papers in the drawer. All of a sudden, you feel his hand on your ankle. Was it an accident? It doesn't move—it stays there, as if waiting for some kind of response. After an uncomfortably long pause, you feel his hand creep up your leg and then stop again. You decide you like it.

Before very long his hand is between your legs playing against your panties, over the lips of your cunt. You don't skip a letter in a determined effort not to attract attention in the office.

Now he's managed to reach your wet cunt and has begun inserting his fingers in and out, very slowly. You try not to give a clue to the below-desk activity, but it's getting more difficult. He increases the tempo now, moving his fingers quicker and quicker. You reach in back of you, searching for his penis. He helps you by unzipping his fly. Your fingers wrap around his shaft, and you start playing with him. You're still facing the opposite direction, typing with one hand. You jerk him rapidly, and inside your cunt, his hand keeps time.

It only takes a little more of his rubbing before you have a very enjoyable orgasm. In a moment he zips up his pants, stands up, and walks back into his office. You smooth down your skirt and return your full attention to your work.

110. Male participation in work as a defense against mother (woman): In another Mike Nichols and Elaine May skit called "Mother and Son," we have a humorous portrayal of what happens to a son when his mother doesn't recognize his awesome accomplishments in his work world. The son is a nuclear scientist specializing in sending up rockets, surely an undertaking sufficient to inspire maternal awe and the recognition that in life's accomplishments he far surpasses her. But no. "I read in the paper how you keep losing them (rockets)," the mother says to her son on the phone. He becomes exasperated, crying, "I don't lose them!" To which she returns, "I thought, well, what if they're taking it out of his pay." She harangues him about why he hasn't called her, saying "I'm sure all the other

scientists there find the time, after count-off." He bellows out a correction of her mistaken term, "Countdown!" Not until he has been reduced to a goo-goo ga-ga baby does she hang up the phone. Rather than a real-life portrayal of the Jewish mother, this is a portrayal of the little's boy's fear of her.

111. From a scene titled "Your Resume's Most Impressive:"

> "Your resume's most impressive."
> "Oh do you really?"
> "Think."
> "So?"
> "Yes."
>
> "You think my resume's?"
> "Most impressive."
> "Do you?"
> "Really."
> "Think?"
> "So?"
> "Yes."
>
> "Yes it's quite long."
> "And impressive?"
> "Sleek and golden."
> "Most impressive?"
> "Your resume, yes."

"Oh I'm so glad you said so. I'm so glad you said yes. I tried so hard to make you say just that. Yes."

"How's that?"

"Well I worked see. In all these places. To make you see."

"Just that?"

"Oh yes. I worked so hard here and I worked so hard there and I worked everywhere I could doing whatever I could for whatever I could. I mean for pay. It looks longer that way."

"Your resume's most impressive. Sleek and golden. Long and golden. Not too fat."

"Oh yes I worked very hard on that too. To make it seem not too fat. I exercised it every day."

"Your resume's most impressive. Long and

sleek. Not too fat. Toned just right. I like it this way."

"Oh yes. I worked very hard on that. Only took it out at night so it stayed that way. No sun. Toned right."

"But it is golden. Golden right. Pale gold tone. Right just right."

"Well yes it is a bit golden because though I only took it out at night to keep it from the sun it has taken on its own heated tone from sweating inside during the days when I stay with it typing it over and over to get it just right. It gets heated up from being warmed over that way."

"Well, if we want any long skinny blonds, we'll let you know."

"This job's for research you know."

"Yes we know. Now go."

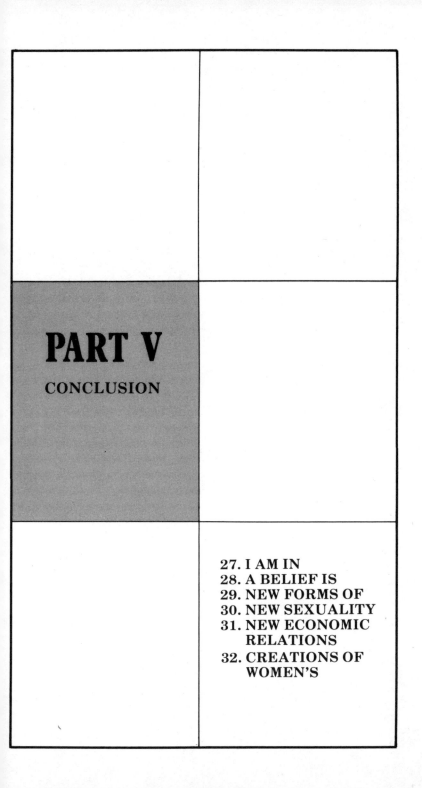

PART V

CONCLUSION

27.

I AM IN New England. Standing by the root of a tree looking up. Musing about how the mind is like a tree, having so many roots and branches. My eye follows a branch out and returns to the trunk; moves up; repeats the process. Many branches out; return; up—over and over. And on each branch so many twigs groping out. Amazing, lying on one's back and looking up, that trees stand at all. That anyone does. That the energy is always up.

I was searching for the answer so long I forgot the question. Year ago set out from the midwest in my van. Looking at communes, women's lands, writing and re-writing the book, seeking the transcendent, the spiritual, the utopia on earth. A way to survive. The festivals. Kept writing all along.

It doesn't exist. Been doing healings on everyone else but myself. Finally did. Remembered when I was thinking of going into standup comedy advocating oblivion and transcendence to blot out the pain of understanding. Having given up comfort. Ha ha ha. At the end of two theory books turn to drink. Drugs. Now it's nature and meditation. Heal with sound. Song. When everyone must ask "what's the next project?" Gulp—last spring I was really answering "trying not to become an alcoholic." Crestfallen looks on peoples' faces, in the universities, in the cities, honest but glib.

Ah hah—another flash—on the floor in a boarding-house. 66 green. An UNDERSTANDING. Creating more reasons to block out the pain. The crestfallen disillusion. As male religions make something dirty and negative out of the female body, so do the women's religions out of "male energy," men. The vision from the midwest a year ago seems wrong. I can't streamline myself, take the chaps and stirrups off, wear down the edges. I don't fit in. The mind races too fast. And the racing intellectual clicking mind has been dubbed the mind of men. So, anarchy and freedom. The freedom to wander and roam. To come down wherever you want and make that home. To accept connections wherever they come. When you fly there are so few of them.

There is a cognitive basis behind all the magical and mystical. As scientific as capitalism and as anarchistic as socialism. Or is it the other way around? My mind is like a forest full of trees. How painful. Back to civilization and it's walk on the ordered sidewalks please.

Some of the consciousness shared in the networks grounds, supports and illustrates theory in fact deepening the validity of the organized perceptions and enriching them greatly. For example, the *Daughter* who is a survivor of incest tends to rove around a lot from place to place (familiar to our reader under *Daughter*'s relationship to work) and to feel safer in public exposed places rather than in her own space in which she has no recourse to anyone if she should be invaded (*Daughter* never gets a space to call her own—another *Daughter* workplace characteristic). She has also experienced protecting herself from an assaultive demeaning unsafe reality by leaving her body—disappearing, leaving few traces, rebelling like an angry *Daughter* whose consciousness conjured up in defiance is her only mantle between herself and a structure which cancels and threatens her very existence. Remember the woman in the credit department of a major store who faked accents?

Another *Daughter* workplace characteristic which the reader might recall is not being structured into working relations which require cooperation with co-workers (rote stamp-licking versus cooperation in team work of *Brother*, assembly line or fireman's chain). Well if the people nearest you as a child were throwing you off slide sets, down stairways, torturing and then molesting you sexually, it is difficult to be cooperative with those who are in close quarters to you. Thus you get a *Daughter*'s rather than *Sister*'s consciousness if the childhood molester was not father or uncle but sibling as a high proportion are.

And, the incest survivor is likely to flee when she feels caved in or endangered, hence *Daughter* doesn't get benefits of full time employment or advantages of staying in one workplace long enough.

Furthermore, women whose bodies have been assaulted at an early age tend to stay at that age of development psychically even though their bodies age. Others see them as young, childlike, irresponsible—and we know that the *Daughter*'s job has no responsibility in the workplace structure at all.

Incest survivors also tend to get into masochistic experiences which the *Daughter*'s job definitely is: accepting rote commands, shutting up and doing what you are told—the nugget of the early rape and violence experience which led to going dead or numb and feeling defenseless as no one would believe her if she told, much less take her seriously. This also corresponds to being low on the material reward side—if you are raped and battered as a child it is hard to ever have the sense that you are worth anything throughout the rest of your life.

Although I am severely tempted, I am not going to write extensively about consciousness raised in this direction which happened to me, I must admit, after I wrote most of the material in this book. But if an incest survivor support group should take the workplace paradigm section of this book, and disregard the derivation from Freudian categories which members might find offensive, I am sure there would be many many more parallels between the *Daughter*'s consciousness at work specifically and the survivor's consciousness generally.*

It might even be an asset if such a group were to do this work, not only in terms of contribution to social theory but in terms of clarifying grounds for practice in all-women's situations. Even when men are taken out of the picture, class, status and power lines develop internally in all-women's communities and working situations. For example, on most of the women's lands there is a division between Gypsies (*Daughters*) and Crones (mothers

*Thanks to Myra L. Liane and Valerie Heller

even after leaving the patriarchal structure as *Wives*.) Frequently there is not much understanding between these two groups and certainly not much understanding of the roving consciousness of the *Daughter*/Gypsy (who become the landless consciousness of the Crones, who are as the landskeeper or landed aristocracy.) Stars and planet configurations explain much of this to their own inhabitants but so does this unique workplace relations theory when tied to developments in the incest survivors movement. As to the relation to class, usually Crones are upwardly mobile working class women and the Gypsies are downwardly mobile middle class women, when we are talking about class as defined by ties to points in the patriarchy at birth (*Father*).

28.

A BELIEF IS like a cloak, you put it on when you need it (or) The Truth Is There Is No Truth, so what do we need to believe in now?

I was on my way to the desert for the solstice. But instead I hopped a plane to the Northeast.

In limbo between San Francisco and New York. Berkeley/Boston. Up in the air I have a vision of this book's structure, like a Hindu Raga. Start with the drone. Gradually add sound, rhythm. Go off in all the improvisations. The return to the home base. The simple drone— what note to end on—what tone—

Let's put it this way folks—I was about to go find cosmic lady and get on the space ship with her—but remembered I had to proof this end. Met many street philosophers in Berkeley, of which she is one. I stalked the streets in my robes, and the bicyclers appreciated my wisdom...Looking down on planet earth, what do we do *that this cycle goes on and on...*

I had a vision once wandering into the balcony of the New York Stock Exchange, in the artists' financial neighborhood. Before the rich people chased us out, I'd stroll for distraction from writing and watch the action. Of course, I'd see other than the material plane. The balcony straight across from me was filled with rows of men and women receiving phone calls from stock owners and investors all over the world; and likewise calling to report the news of the processes on the floor. Then, with appropriate decisions, input and answers, those on the balcony directly across would send pages or runners to the floor to put up certain bids or amounts at each appropriate stall or receptacle whenever commodities were being exchanged or auctioned off.

I saw no reason why an economy with such an elaborate communications system could not be subverted appropriately to achieve the desired effect. The first step would be the realignment of pooling income lines in the following way: the sex and age groupings to be the new economic basis would be formed by death and birth until all individual owners of cash, money and survival resources had died off. Every year when all the old men died (Rockefellers to Bowery Bums) all would dissolve their income and wealth to the baby boys born that year. Likewise, with dying women and baby girls. Of course some adjustments to equalize would be made. The inheritance of the baby males would be taxed by the baby girls until all the previous elders/owners had died off. The tax would be 46%, to correct the economic wrongs and remnants of the past in which women had been earning 54¢ to each dollar earned by men. Some other tax would have to be levied, since women now only own 10% of the world's productive resources and wealth—so 90% of the dying men's wealth and resources transferred to the inheritance funds of the boys born in each year would get transferred to the girls born in the same year, thus equalizing what goes to boys and girls from the dying old men and women

And the vision continued...Then there would be a system like citibank punch-in bank accounts, where people could withdraw from and deposit to these joint accounts all over the world, wherever they were, as earned, acquired or needed. Through these accounts people would control daily survival and earnings; through such an organization as the stock exchange investment decisions would be made by each grouping; thus each grouping would be determining new directions for the overall economic growth of the world and the nation. Instead of arguing about the importance of day care over wars, each group in the anarchy of the free market system, bidding against each other as sex and age groups, could determine what was economically feasible and do it.

Of course this vision abstracts greatly from the practical details; and hence the politics and economics against enacting it are severe; leading it to be dismissed as utopian by some but also to be inspiring to others. It was a personal vision, not aligned with actual attempts in the U.S., although in countries such as the Netherlands many economic re-shufflings occur through the central government to channel income this way and that, until all individuals are taken care of and poverty is eliminated. It is possible to rethink economic pooling lines, with a sufficiently macro-tinkering mind. And access to a state ready and willing to do it.

Nonetheless, until this is enacted on a world order with coordinating councils on a regional basis—is there anything closer to home base which can be done? This is not a book of strategy, but I do want to sketch recent directions that women have been employing to counteract the family/work/family cycle without delving too deeply into the further complications that arise resisting change in dimensions in which it is needed and to see what would be necessary to get to the steps of enacting that rather large scale utopian vision.

29.
NEW FORMS OF consciousness. Consciousness would have to be jolted out of family roles to accomplish the vision. Since your spirit comes into your body in this lifetime and is immediately situated in a family, and the family situation defines the consciousness that is kept intact to get people to work,it seems important to create structures in which freer spirits—not trapped in distorting sex and age roles—can get out.

I began to be a serious participant in this process backwards. I was doing research for a community mental health center on the effects of institutionalization. In this society, people are often institutionalized if they are out of their bodies, not properly socialized, and do not fit into "civilized" (barbarically crippling) slots. Frequently, those defined by their families or employers at work. On this job

I was reading *The Manufacture of Madness* by Thomas Szasz. In this book he made an analogy between the fifteenth century witch and the twentieth century mental patient. The mental "health" system functions now to persecute those who are threatening to the society, as witches were in the analogous era. I thought perhaps I had an affinity with witches and began to explore that area. The same summer I read the book, I went to the Michigan Women's Music Festival, a gathering of 7,000 women camping out, participating in cooperative work exchange relationships and political workshops. Seeking an alternative to the psychology and psychiatry which generate and reinforce a family consciousness, I went to a workshop conducted by Z Budapest, a leader in the growing feminist spirituality movement. I asked her to cast a spell on me. She said she preferred I do it myself. I went away cursing darts, you even have to be politically correct in the religions of this movement.

From the beginning section of this book, the reader can see I was always deeply affected by spirituality and rituals; and that in fact I had had outer-body experiences such as described in the rape account; we even went into how these experiences affected the theory I later developed and presented in this book. The point is not just my personal history, but how I learned from the impact of traditional religions on my own belief system and hence sought development of new ones, especially as my own drop in economic position brought me out of the realm of expensive feminist/Freudian therapy. Then the sources of support I sought were different—those which women of poorer classes were accustomed to: the black "soul" singers and sisters. I defined spirituality as the breaking down of individual boundaries, the pooling of collective consciousness particularly through artistic and physical work and thus saw the interactions of women in Michigan engaging in spiritualized rituals as seeming to offer suggestions about what must be done to substitute new ideas in place of traditional cultural indoctrinations. Z's desire to have each woman take charge of her own experience also indicated that the feminist spiritual forms being developed also challenged traditional religion's top-down hierarchical habits.

The psychiatry and psychology for which I was seeking alternatives are like traditional religion: top-down, with authority figures offering hopes and illusions in exchange for payment and obedience. You speak, or confess, and a therapist or psychiatrist tells you "you are borderline," "you are acting out," "you are this or that." The effect is that you start seeing in yourself what you are told to see, and you look backwards to blame the family and interactions in early childhood, if not yourself. As being salvaged by the new feminist spirituality movement, witchcraft implants positive forward-looking images instead. Compare, for example, the Rorschach test, psychiatry's implement, to Tarot readings, a feminist tool. In the Rorschach test the psychologist shows you a stack of pictures and asks for your interpretation. Then he or she goes away, and interprets or diagnoses the result although not necessarily to be shared with you. He or she gets a static statement of what kind of "aberrant personality" you manifest. A Tarot reading on the other hand is done by another individual on a par with you who likewise shows you various images. She or he involves you in interpreting the images, however, and both of you know it is an interaction in the moment, in the process. The result will be different the next throw. The Rorschach symbols and Tarot cards are each props, or tools. The former is used to observe the individual, label her or him, isolate her or him, all from a position of authority. The latter, however, are an aid feminists use to provoke new associations and ideas.

There are forms of psychology which utilize some of the ritualized group aspects: co-counseling, for example, which stresses the importance of present time, light and lively, news and goods shared among participants and the idea that any co-counselor can counsel for another, the feudal idea of non-monetary trade. But all of the psychological focus tends to be on understanding—as if understanding heals instead of being so painful as to drive one towards obliteration—death, drink, drugs. I am not going to discuss and defend the whole new age component, of which the many many feminist spirituality leaders are merely a part: Starhawk, Shetinah Mountain Water, Diane Seagull, etc., etc., or debate the relevancy and reality of the magical and the mystical, but just say that it is possible to change one's stance towards the world through learning to trust intuitive power, practicing yoga which places you in a mountain warrior stance, calming yourself and your inner being with sound, color, nature, candles, and even the images of the tarot which appeal to the lower recesses of the mind and offer an alternative refocus for it. Psychology and psychiatry as practiced today ripped off witchcraft, retaining only the ritual of confession but stripping it of all the comforting trapping and focusing it on an all-knowing doctor. All the collective consciousness-pooling intrinsic to the old pagentry was removed. Those involved in creating new rituals, especially ones that cast a different spectre about the power of women, give us inputs of different kinds of values. To receive these we must strip out the indoctrinated prejudice in the form of stereotypes of charlatan gypsy fortune tellers and green-faced witches on brooms stirring demons in poisonous brews from our minds. Those images themselves—caricatures—were developed as part of the war against the wisdom that women had *and are reclaiming again* to fight against the evils of civilization and an overly complex society.

The further one explores this area, the less "magical and mystical" it becomes. There is a science behind all of it: the creation of different alpha/beta/theta conscious states, and the susceptibility for reprogramming that any human mind can contain. Also, the drum beats, and wearing no clothes in outdoor circles, can make spirits soar out of bodies and encircle with each other in aura swirls. The power is incredible, and the only word to call it is magical, meaning a suspension of disbelief and participation in the unknown, a magical experience of altered states of consciousness. In Michigan this year, many women participated in an Amazon Warrior circle, in which all of us said a chant and each of us took turns to get in the circle and say a song or tale about how we had conquered something in our lives. The powerful effect is strong: to have to tell a story of how you are strong instead of the constant victimization and experience of the weak. Part of the requirement is also that you sing, and move as you talk, and raise your voice and you can even gesture and shake and *scream*. This definitely changes the civilized, socialized slots, or causes one to push at one's boundaries. At the end when you throw in a piece of clothing and dance back out, with everyone chanting for you, you *do* feel strong; and you are put in touch with powers you might not know about. Much more empowering than recounting one's life individually to a therapist, and being told "you are trying to get somebody to mother you," "that is appropriate to the situation, this is not," etc. And women reclaiming, recreating these rituals, *are* strong as women of color have found these religious, gospel experiences, laying on of hands, speaking in tongues, strengthening over the years. Thus, by learning to recreate the childish sense of vulnerability, and groping for new images in this aesthetic and tribal mode of experience, we might get the emotional strength needed to carry out survival and collective politics.

30.
NEW ECONOMIC RELATIONS. So we have a glimpse how it is possible to change consciousness. But what about breaking down the economic lines described in the book? Once we change consciousness, it will not be very likely that we can operate immediately that vision of sex and age re-pooling plan. First what would be necessary would be a series of smaller units trying to enact changes. These would be the cooperative units, much as some of the Eastern European socialistic states have cooperation among worker-controlled and managed factories. We do have little indigenous societies across the United States and we can look at them in terms of finding something a bit more hopeful. Convinced that large-scale social reorganization of production by socialist revolutions did not help much because of the continuation of economic pooling arrangements through the family what do the intentional utopian communities that are run acording to an economic plan have to teach us about our own future and possibilities on a smaller scale? Because even if not self-defined as socialist, they do have internal economic systems generated to enact different values.

These intentional communities have always existed in the United States, such as the Shaker communities, and others formed with a religious utopian base. By

.looking at these contemporary utopian communities, we could still pursue the question that if the problems are socially based, as says feminist social theory, (whether marxist, socialist/feminist, or liberal or radical feminist) and if the theory presented in this book is correct, how are people in more controlled and limited situations able to break the cycle? Can we see how these small groups inspired to create pockets of changed economic relations with a collective organization of production and consumption, and inputs of new cultural values, are able to break down both the economic basis for the nuclear family and the division of labor by sex and age at work?

Let's look at a few which are still heterosexual (mixed) to see how far changes can be made without use of a revolutionary sexuality to undermine the "natural" income poolings and sex and age divisions in society.

One of the most well known and economically viable of these cooperative economic institutions, The Farm, in Tennesee, has single family units but common development and child care. Children can by choice move in with different adults. Household chores are collectivized, and all pool money. In work arrangements, an emphasis is maintained on the interchangeability of persons. No person is indispensably attached to a particular job—i.e., its member say there is no *Father* workplace character. There is encouragement that no person hold a job for more than five years; and an economic planning council made up mostly of women and teenagers. This group counterbalances, and makes sure that economic decisions are not made on the basis of profit alone.

The commune, of course, is still limited by the outer environment, and in hearing this argument one is reminded of the early debates about economic planning which occurred in the Soviet Union. Internal socialistic relations had to be postponed, it was argued, because the economy at large had to interact or trade with the world-wide capitalist order. The women, similarly, maintain that a six person all women auto crew cannot be sent to outlying areas to work on cars, because the outside jobs are given by sex-role conservative people. In spite of the external pressure for sex and age divisions to exist, internally, the women have developed mechanisms of support for each other which are possible because of everyone living in community rather than privatized families. For example, if a woman is getting a hard time from "her man," (language is still traditional and colloquial) a group of women may go surround the couple to support her and attack the male, reminiscent of African tribes.

Twin Oaks in Virginia, another of the most long lasting and successful cooperative economic organizations is more successful in breaking down nuclear family arrangements. Its 70 people form an overall consumption unit, with each person participating in an elaborate labor credit system. No circulation of money occurs, and everyone moves around from task to task. Much of "housework" or "consumption work" traditionally carried out by women, both in the family and the outside world, is instead incorporated into the labor plan. By this system what has not been possible in communes in existing socialist countries is achieved. And although it is continually evolving, communal childrearing also breaks down the basis for many psychologically debilitating interactions.

Again, the systemic unit is not perfect, and one gets the sense that what exists now in terms of coupledom, childrearing and workplace relations is much more conservative than 15 years ago when the commune began. Attitudes expressed by the old guard, for example, now include favoring of specialization, when job rotation was a principle in the early days. Those who have been there longer argue that efficiency is desirable, due to problems of wasted time created by constant turnover. Therefore in terms of changing patriarchal work relations, a continuous struggle remains, and cultural inputs designed to change consciousness are still an important factor. But, in any case, these experiments certainly have a lot to teach about the possibility of escaping the circle of socialization and oppression through localized gains even while we also fight—hopefully guided by new, rather than habitualized ideas—for broad social change as well.

Again, to return to our vision, all the same sex and age group members could meet internally in the collective unit and plug into the regional convention of everyone in the same grouping: to get strength for struggling internally, and to participate by group in the sex and age outer coordinating state system. Then everyone coming to the community and within it would be equally endowed with resources, have access to investment in desired directions, etc.

31.

NEW SEXUALITY. As already indicated in the course of our discussions, a revolutionary sexuality may also be an effective tool in breaking the cycle of socialization and work role habituation. It would be nice to think that anything that subverts sex roles, for example, everything in gay culture, would be revolutionary. But that is not so, as "straight" gayness does little removed from a political context, and sexual preference does not guarantee a political analysis.

It is interesting, however, that in the community movement striving towards new economic relationships described above, a split-off occurred. Women left the mixed cooperative movement on the ideological belief that the problem is not social, but biological. Women taking this position have evolved the philosophy that everything must be done to stay away from the contamination of male energies; even to the point of staying away from women who are contaminated by male energy, male thinking, male perspectives.

What I am describing is the frontier of lesbian separatism, in self-description, the nucleus for the lesbian separatist economy. These farms, insofar as they work, are the practical application of pooling income theory, the closest we can approximate to it in the 1980s United States. Although ideal proponents of the plan, the women in these communities would probably not want to participate because the coordination would require coordination with men, straight women, women influenced by male philosophy, etc. My vision, or the one originally proposed, was not separatist per se, in that the overall machinations still had something to do with men; these women go back to the source and intend to build up their own economy. This seems extreme, even in some cases moving to a development of alternate power systems and a severance from ties to patriarchal electricity—but, indeed, this is a choice: we can remain marginal to the dominant culture, and even to the counterculture; or we can create centers of our own new culture, going back to the source and building up an economic basis for the channeling of new energies, and the creation of new images. In this perspective, "coming out" as a lesbian would be an erroneous concept; a better phrase would be "coming in" to a new kind of society.

The models used in the women's farm movement vary from matriarchy to cooperative, but are still plagued by class divisions brought from the outside. The hope is that patriarchal economic and workplace relations as described in this book not be reproduced. Due to the self-same problems that women face in the larger economy, I haven't yet located a farm with sufficient economic development to analyze the work relations to see how they would apply or transcend the four categories devised in this book. Members in the ones I have visited are still dependent on the government, outside jobs, and class-based familial sources, until they learn to develop their own industries. Some have individuals producing crafts to sell at fairs; in most trades and exchanges are developed which allow an economic existence outside the money economy; and some grow some food to eat and to exchange with the outside world on a very minimal basis.

We can hope that these experiments will have a head start in the effort to create social forms which don't replicate the familiar patterns. But until there is a real self sufficient basis this is an abstract hope to hold to the women's land world. Many are busy recovering from a plagued existence, and plaguing each other with internal horizontal hostility problems.

The roles that do occur seem to do so in different forms: butch/femme, gypsy/crone, aquarius/virgo; material plane person/spiritually enlightened. Perhaps these are all mother/daughter roles, sensed in other gestalts. The roles that do occur can certainly be seen at the women's music festivals, discussed earlier, where the mini-creation of an all women's world—and the political struggles over it—happen very fast. It is there perhaps that the most lessons can be learned rather than per se on the women's lands themselves.*

---

*See my writing on politics of the festivals in *Big Mama Rag* and on the women's farms and Twin Oaks in Ruby Dorlich, editor, forthcoming: *The Search for Utopia: What Do Women Want?*

32.

CREATION OF WOMEN'S Culture. In the economic sense, then, these farms might not yet be an alternative. However, they are interesting in terms of culture as a political/sociological phenomenon potentially serving the same purpose for women, for example, that the kibbutzim of Israel serve for Jews—whatever one may think about the Israeli State.

Both groups, those who advocate the new cultures for women and those who do so for Jews—have the view that each group is an endangered species being persecuted by a dominant culture, and kept marginal to the economy by a history and present of discrimination; and that the antidote to victimization is to pioneer, to build up from scratch, to learn what each has been kept ignorant of— use of tools, survival skills, self-defense.

The most vocal advocates of these positions—lesbian separatists for women, and Zionists for Jews—feel the political economic necessity to create a home or refuge, a place where it is safe to be free from the strictures and prejudices of the dominant culture.

Both had their origins in being disillusioned with the ability of other revolutionary tendencies to place overcoming their specific group's economic marginality into account in general economic planning. As the women's farm movement grew out of women's dissatisfaction with the male counterculture's planning for economic self-sufficiency, so did the socialistic kibbutz movement of Zionism grow out of Jews' disappointments with the continuation of pogroms and Jewish persecution after the overthrow of the Czar in Soviet Russia.

The relative success of the kibbutzim in comparison to the women's farms comes not from a longer history of persecution, but, among Jews, a longer tradition of self-organization, a less-than-fledgling status, a greater access to material resources, and a more powerful religion and history of songs, dance, ritual, and systems of cohering around common visions and values: hence the importance of consciousness change described in the first section of this chapter.

So far I have talked about the political creation of lesbians and the way anti-semitism creates the Jew, and this seems like a negative push, overlooking the positive

pull of culture and likeness which draws people together...
choosing to associate with the "like," rather than seeking
out disorienting involvement with the "other." I have not
talked about the pitfalls: the problems which occur when
an oppressed group develops its own norms in the name of
freedom and then proceeds to impose those norms in a
repressive way on each other. The nuclei of these communities can become conformist, rigid, and not accepting of
differences which stem from different positions in the
culture.

In many ways the separatist tendency has begun to
create a women's culture and to create an environment in
which the positive cultural aspect can flourish. Thus the
women's communities have begun adopting their own
forms similar to the various ways of creating Jewish
culture—the selection of their own names which identify
participants with a political, ethnic, or tribal membership; wearing of political insignias; adopting special
dietary habits; promoting community solidarity and
sharing; holding community rituals, and holidays which
separate particiants from cycles and seasons celebrated
by the dominant culture.

In any case, as with experiments in new economic
forms, likewise for experiments in new cultural forms: of
course there are many pitfalls, but the impetus and
potential is positive. We wanted to see what smaller
cooperative units might be linked and coordinated to
facilitate the global macro re-pooling concept. We found
that to really do that we have to have the strength to
develop new forms of consciousness; and that nuclei exist
to form the facilitating basis. But those small nuclei that
do exist get involved in the necessary first step: creation of
cohering culture, and problems arise with that. Perhaps
they need the economic re-alignment to happen first—to
provide them with the resources to develop the new economic basis. Until such time, they will exist to help us open
our minds to new ways and we must listen to the utopias
in our dreams and not be afraid of visions, visionaries,
ideas and practices in this important transitional time as
the material plane cracks and crumbles across the entire
planet. With our souls leading, we can free our spirits to
redirect, put bāck into the planet, into each other and into
ourselves.

TEIKYO WESTMAR UNIV. LIBRARY

HD 6060 .W45 1983
Weinbaum, Batya.
Pictures of patriarchy
        (92-1825)

DEMCO